T0339548

Buying Complex IT Systems

Many of us have experience of using IT systems at work that just don't work right or cause more problems than they solve. Even if we've been lucky at work and always had the opportunity to use well-built and functional IT systems, it's common to hear in the press or in our day-to-day lives about IT systems that are "down" or "slow", or just do not work right. While it can be inconvenient to have to use IT systems that aren't the best for businesses, buying an IT system that isn't fit for its intended purpose can have devastating effects on the business itself and the careers of the people involved. The senior team of any business will know everything there is to know about their specific business or market, but their job is not to implement IT systems. This brings an inherent unfairness to IT systems procurement because it makes it very easy to buy the wrong thing at the wrong price. In essence, the buyers are amateurs but the sellers are professionals. This mismatch is at the root cause of the majority IT systems failures – a problem which might cost a company millions and have other negative impacts. This book is intended to be a practical manual for senior leaders in small-to-medium businesses that will teach them how to buy IT systems effectively – i.e. to somewhat transform the non-IT senior leadership personnel such that they are more informed and capable buyers. There are a million-and-one potholes that can trip up a business, even when buying from an otherwise effective and reputable seller, and this book looks to make it far more likely that the reader will buy the right system, at the right price. The author uses his extensive experience to highlight problem areas and offer solutions to eliminate them.

Buying Complex IT Systems

Computer System Procurement for Non-Technical Managers

Matthew Reynolds

Routledge
Taylor & Francis Group

A PRODUCTIVITY PRESS BOOK

First published 2024
by Routledge
605 Third Avenue, New York, NY 10158

and by Routledge
4 Park Square, Milton Park, Abingdon, Oxon, OX14 4RN

Routledge is an imprint of the Taylor & Francis Group, an informa business

ISBN: 978-1-032-54849-4 (hbk)
ISBN: 978-1-032-54848-7 (pbk)
ISBN: 978-1-003-42776-6 (ebk)

DOI: 10.4324/9781003427766

Typeset in Garamond
by MPS Limited, Dehradun

Contents

Introduction

This is a book about software.

The title of the book talks about computer and IT systems, but regardless of what you buy, if you're buying information technology, in reality, you are buying software. You may happen to have to buy some hardware to go along with it (laptops, printers, phones, servers, etc.), but all the actual value – the reason why you are shelling out the cash – comes from the software.

Regardless of what sort of computer you are using – an actual laptop, your smartphone, a chip and PIN card reader, the engine control unit in your car, the internet-connected CCTV camera on the front of your house, all of the value – the benefit you derive from having it – comes from the software, and just the software.

This concept is so important that we start this book with a "Chapter Zero", designed to help you – the reader – get to grips with it before we go on and start talking about buying whatever IT system your business needs. So, let's get on with it.

Zeroes and Ones

You are likely familiar with the concept that computers work on binary code – zeroes and ones. The reason for this is that the computers that we use day-to-day are electrical devices and any given circuit can either be on (a "one") or off (a "zero"). Somehow we are able to get from this basic premise to the day-to-day experiences that we have of using software, whether that's sending a message on WhatsApp, watching a YouTube video, or using some operational system in our organisation. Next, I have to teach you how to write software...

(You may well find that the system you commission does not involve you directly or indirectly writing software – most systems involve buying some prewritten software and deploying it. However, the premise of this book is that in my experience, people who know how IT systems are built tend to be better at buying IT systems as they are more able to control risk around the procurement process.)

To start building software, the first thing you need is an idea. This in itself is a sufficiently important concept that we spent a lot of Chapter 1 looking at just that. For the purposes of this exercise, we need to imagine that the business has identified a need that can be met with some computer system (i.e. software). Again for this exercise, we are going to imagine that the business wants a system that allows employees to submit expense claims. The ultimate goal is that the employee can log in, submit a claim, and (if the claim is valid) find themselves reimbursed for that payment.

So we know roughly what we want to try to deliver with our new IT system, and we know that computers work in zeros and ones/binary code. In terms of scope, we have one sentence with three subclauses, and we have to turn that a string of zeroes and ones that are in exactly the right order in order that we can "realise" this IT system and have our staff use it.

The process that happens here is one of continuous "decomposition". We take our one concept and keep dividing it down into small and smaller parts until eventually we have decomposed the concept into a piece of software that can be installed and operated. (This is also why earlier I said the hardware wasn't important – we can run that software pretty much on anything we like, and there are a handful of novel decisions that we need to make in terms of choosing hardware, but there are tens of thousands of novel decisions that we need to make in order to build the software.)

The general shape of the decomposition that we need to go through is as follows – and we'll be going through this structure throughout the book, but don't worry as we will be going into a lot of detail on these points in later chapters:

■ Concept – a high-level description of what we are trying to achieve,

■ Outline requirements – the high-level description decomposed down into a sort of "heads of agreement" that roughly describes the scope of work to be done,

■ Functional specification – the outline requirements decomposed down into a detailed technical document that describes how the system will "function",

■ User stories – at this point, we have a division of labour between the "business" team and the "technical" team. Up to and including the functional specification, the focus has been on business requirements. We now have the technical team take over and the process here is to take the functional specification and turn it into "user stories", these being roughly quasi-narrative descriptions of how each smaller part of the system will be delivered,

■ Tasks – once the user stories have been agreed, they are decomposed into tasks and distributed to whatever "technician" is doing the work. We'll usually call these "engineers" in the book,

■ Source code – this is the actual "code" part that technicians write as part of the implementation. This is where the building part happens – everything prior to this has just been design.

■ Machine code – these are the zeroes and ones that we spoke about at the start. The transformation to source code to machine code is a purely mechanical process. Conceptually, it's the equivalent of waiting for concrete to set once it has been poured. The source code stage of engineers writing software is like pouring concrete – the engineers' work is done, but the concrete is no use until some other "mechanical" process happens.

As we'll also see as we go through the book, to move down through the stages there has to a signoff process of some description. In reality, this whole process and other ancillary processes that we'll see as we go through ***should*** be quite heavy in paperwork, but it's often the case that paperwork/signoff stages are skipped. (By way of a quick hint, try not to skip paperwork.)

Figure 0.1 restates the stages above in diagrammatic form. A key concept is that as we go down through the stages, the "domain technical knowledge" decreases and "IT technical knowledge" increases. We will talk a lot about this idea of "domain". What this means is the collection of "stuff" that you know about because you know your business. I know nothing about – picking a random example – compliance and regulations governing consumer finance agreements, i.e. I know nothing about that "domain", but a compliance officer working for the business regulated by the UK's Financial Conduct Authority will know a lot about that "domain". Similarly, I know nothing about manufacturing the foam used in car seats, but there will be people out there who understand that domain thoroughly.

The point is that in order to design the solution, you do need to have deep and thorough domain knowledge, but you don't necessarily need to know a great deal about IT – you just need to know the right amount to know that you are making competent decisions. Conversely, the engineers need to have deep and throughout technical execution skills, but need domain knowledge deep enough only to know whether

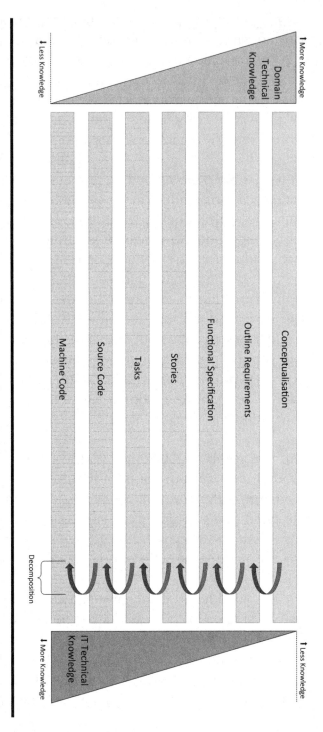

Figure 0.1 How domain knowledge and technical knowledge maintains proportionate importance as the project is developed.

they are or are not making competent decisions as they implement the solution.

This last point is the main reason why I wrote this book – decision makers can find themselves making the wrong decisions, even in groups, around IT systems procurement because they don't know enough about the technical process involved. Raise that knowledge up (even just a little), and you see fewer failed projects, or even fewer projects that just don't deliver the value that it was thought they would do.

"Building Castles in the Sky with Your Mind"

At this point, I've taken you through the rough process of how we take an idea and go through a collection of stages in order to turn that idea into software. We now need to concentrate on the actual "engineering software" part – more specifically, why this is so hard to do and why it so often goes wrong. (Again, as all IT systems are essentially just "applied software", if we understand how the engineering process can go wrong, we can understand why the whole systems delivery piece goes wrong and – ideally – avoid issues.)

All software, regardless of what it is doing, works in exactly one way and one way only. It takes some data as input, runs some operation/operations on that data, and produces a different version of that data as output. This applies on the macro level as well as the micro level. To give some realism to this, imagine you are buying a Diet Coke from the supermarket. At the self-checkout, you scan the barcode – this is the input. Some software runs and the product is added to your bill, and the total cost of your transaction is displayed on the screen (the output). Within that process, there are scores of smaller processes that work together to actually achieve that. That smaller piece is also "orchestrated" within a far larger collection of systems – some to allow the supermarket to account for the transaction, but also orders to go off to the supplier, which in turns then triggers orders from the supplier's suppliers for raw materials, and so on.

The problem to the people building any of this stuff is that none of it is real. The Diet Coke in your hand is real. The till is real. Some would argue the money that you used to pay for it is not real – but there is a tremendous amount of stuff in that process and all the interrelated processes that physically does not exist. The exist only as patterns of electrons representing circuits being on or off – zeros and ones.

When you build something in the real world, physical laws apply. This sets considerable limits on what you can build, how you build it, and how much it costs. Imagine you are doing a DIY project at home and need some wood, and need to cut that wood to a particular length. You have to go and buy the wood, transport it home, prepare to cut it, and cut it. If you cut it in the wrong place, there is no magic undo button, so it's important to get it right the first time. If you're building software, you don't need to buy the wood (you have infinite amounts of it right there, and it's free!), and the measuring it is not that important because if you "cut" it in the wrong place, you can just hit undo. This leads to a highly "experimental" way of approaching problems.

The other problem is that the "big thing" that you are building also doesn't have physical laws to abide by either. If you are building a bridge, there are physical laws that have to be considered – you are generally going to have to use steel and concrete to build the bridge. A software engineer looking to build a bridge might use steel and concrete, but they also may use toothpicks and chewing gum. It gets worse, because it's not necessarily a given that other people looking at the bridge would even be able to tell the bridge was made of toothpicks and chewing gum and would happily drive their car on it as if it were made of steel and concrete. If you make a physical bridge in the real world wrong, it *will* fall down. If you make a software "bridge" in a computer wrong, it *may not* fall down (At least, until one day when it does fall down.) One way to look at it is the physical universe provides an automatic "check and balance" to what you engineer physically, but you don't get that help in software. At this point, you have an engineer that is working in a very experimental way, and is free to build anything that their mind can dream up, without having to worry about the physical universe "telling them off".

The final part of the puzzle is that both the software industry and the IT industry generally lacks a professionalising body. If you want to become a surgeon in the UK, you have to be a member of the Royal College of Surgeons. (Similarly in the USA, you have to be a member of the American College of Surgeons.) This approach is not unusual for professions such a solicitors and barristers (aka lawyers), accountants, nurses – effectively any profession you can think of where *trust* is a key part of the way work is delivered requires a governing body. Yet the IT industry does not have this *requirement*. It's perfectly possible to deliver an IT solution into a business that has devastating financial, commercial, or reputational impact on the client, and there is no oversight. In some rarefied situations, it is possible to cause physical injury or death.

For example, companies producing IT systems related to healthcare delivery in the UK have to adhere to a standard called DCB0129, and adherence to this standard is codified in law (specially the Health and Social Care Act 2012). However, it's up to the commissioning organisation and the supplier to work through these things on an individual, ad hoc basis. There's nothing to stop a supplier taking people straight out of school who don't have degrees, ask them to build a solution, certificate it, and be compliant. Imagine doing that with a group of people, giving them a list of YouTube videos to watch and then handing them a scalpel.

This seems farfetched, but it is analogous to the process that happens in IT systems engineering. Without a professionalising body, there is no governance and outcomes can vary wildly.

At this point we have a discipline that is founded on the idea of experimentation, where the things being dreamt up by the engineer don't have to be constrained by physical laws, and there is virtually no oversight from a professionalising body. Software engineers are, effectively, paid to "build cities in the sky with their minds", and this is generally seen as a beneficial way of doing things. This can lead to some interesting results. On the positive side, it's a hothouse for innovation. The industry is continuously changing and shifting, and we have tools available to us now that were unimaginable even ten years ago. On the negative side, a theme we'll come back to often as we work through the book is that you as a customer need to do work to defend against these biases. This can come as a surprise – no one going into surgery expects to have to ask the surgeon if they've washed their hands, have the equipment, and/or have even attempted the procedure before – but that very much is the case when buying IT systems. You have to develop a kind of "healthy mistrust".

If any of this seems harsh about software engineers, it's not meant to be. I started programming computers when I was eight years old, and I've mucked around with computers in some form or another every single day of my life since. Software engineering is an amazing vocation, hobby, professional, job, or whatever you to call it, and it's amazingly rewarding and fun. But as I've said above, and will say umpteen times as we go forward into the main body of this book – it's tricky to commission IT systems and get the value you want delivered at the price you want to pay.

A Quick Word about "Advice"

I probably should stay right from the beginning – a theme of this book is not just getting a good IT system that suits your needs, but we will also be discussing avoiding legal disputes with suppliers. As well as this, we will often talk about contracts and agreements with suppliers. This all being said, I am not a lawyer, and nothing in this book constitutes legal advice. You should always talk to your own lawyer to get the advice and guidance that you eed.

Author Biography

Matthew Reynolds is a Fractional CTO with 30 years' experience at delivering complex software systems. He's written over a dozen books on software engineering and business, and has previously been a columnist for *The Guardian* newspaper. Today, he's a partner in Forge Startup Studio, a venture studio based in the UK that supports startup and scaleup businesses in delivering their digital solutions. He has a keen interest in technical project remediation and supporting companies who are experiencing challenges or failures with their IT suppliers.

Chapter 1

Going Shopping

This being a book about buying IT systems, in this first chapter, we're going to look at how the business decides that it needs to buy something. In reality, this is more a chapter around how to start building an IT strategy within the organisation. If you're a reader of this book, chances are that you are a non-technical manager embarking on a project that will see the organisation buy a new IT system. One mistake – call it an "opportunity" rather than a "mistake" – that people in that situation sometimes make is to look at that system in isolation, rather than as part of a broader information technology strategy. (And, if you're a non-technical manager heading up this sort of project, you're going to need to get very good at IT strategy, from first principles, quickly.)

Pain Points and Buying Decisions

Being that in 2024 we're not at a point where artificial intelligences are making decisions for us, the decisions that we make both in business and personally are done by human beings – creatures who are emotional in nature. Human decision-making is done on the basis whereby decisions are made emotionally and justified rationally. When it comes to decisions

DOI: 10.4324/9781003427766-1

1

related to purchasing, this means that we will decide to buy something from an emotional place and then back-up and test this decision using some mechanism that checks to see if the decision is rational. When we buy something as a regular consumer (business-to-consumer purchasing), we may find that there is not much rigour to this rational element. When we buy something as a business (business-to-business purchasing), we usually have to justify any decision to the organisation as a whole by applying a business case. This generally means that business-to-business purchasing is regarded as being more rational.

I have spent my career on the "IT supplier" side of the fence. One of my motivations for writing this book was to help customers of IT systems understand the dynamics of what is going on in the supplier's mind. A lot of this book is looking to help you "look behind the curtain", because if you understand both what is happening in your organisation and in the supplier's business, you should get better outcomes. This is not because IT suppliers are out to trick you. IT systems supply operates on a relationship basis – both you and the supplier have to get to know each other extremely well indeed, and you do because, like in any good relationship, if you can both help and support each other, you will both get more out of the relationship. In the context of this business relationship, your goal is to get an IT system that delivers the value you want at the price you want. (Part of that value is to ensure that whatever you buy today is a good foundation for what you want to do tomorrow, but we will get into that as we go on.) So we are going to learn exactly how a typical IT supplier sells and delivers their systems.

This book is notionally going to think about an IT system that is reasonably expensive: £100,000 or around $120,000. You can spend a lot more – you may be thinking about spending a lot more. I've chosen this sum because it's sufficiently large that if the purchase ends up not delivering great value to the organisation, it will certainly be noticed at a senior level, i.e. it's the minimum project size where a mistake is difficult to hide.

In order for a sale of that size to be made, from your side as a customer, there has to be a strong business case, but as we said above, purchasing is initially an emotional decision. Another way to describe this then is that there has to be a sufficiently strong "pain point" within the organisation that a sales offer can hook on to, this sales offer/pain point then being boiled down to something that rationally addresses a business case. It is easier for the supplier to sell into you if the "pain" is stronger. If someone has a broken leg, how much would they pay for a shot of morphine? In that same situation, how much would they pay for a bottle of vitamin C tablets?

From the customer's perspective, you do not want to have a broken leg at all. From the supplier's perspective, their job is easier the worse your pain is. Again, this doesn't mean that suppliers lie, but it does mean that certain products are easier to sell than others. A traditionally easy type of solution to sell into businesses are cybersecurity products; at the time of writing, the easiest subtype of this solution to sell is products that prevent against ransomware attacks. This is because the perceived pain is so high, there's something very obvious for the supplier to "hook" onto. However, most IT solutions sold into businesses are incredibly difficult to sell. For this, you should read in that instead of "difficult to sell", they are "*expensive* to sell".

If you are an IT supplier selling a complex system into a relatively specialised market, the "cost of acquisition" (the amount of money it takes to acquire you as a customer) is eye-watering. In order to sell you a £100k/$120k project, the supplier may well be looking a cost of £10k/$12k just to get you to a point where the contract is signed. Again, there's nothing necessarily wrong with this, but IT systems customers often do not fully appreciate this part of the suppliers' motivation. One problem you can find with this is "bait and switch" – the sales process looks great, but the implementation is quite ropey. (This happens when the supplier 'evolves' to be better at selling than they are at implementing – i.e. they end up being better at finding new customers than they are at retaining existing ones.) Another problem you can find is that the supplier may "spice up" their capabilities around a particular offering and then use your project to learn how to deliver what they said they could initially. We'll look at more problems as we go, but I'm keen to make sure the narrative on this book is about parties genuinely looking to support each other in a win–win. The one unavoidable fallout from the cost of acquisition issue is that the supplier will effectively want to marry you for life. That initial acquisition cost has to be paid back out of profits from very long engagements. This can be positive – it's not unusual for a supplier and customer to work together for 10–20 years, over which time you get a lot of optimisation around delivery and really can work with fantastic synergy. But as well come on to, the supplier's need to make a decent profit out of your project will be a factor throughout.

Finding Your Pain Point

Coming back to this idea about pain. It's important that you don't keep the pain point secret. You're not looking to dance around the solution – the more the supplier knows about your specific pain (and the more they know about your organisation generally) the better your outcomes will be. As such, it's good to (a) be honest and (b) to make expressing your organisational pain something you want to get better at over time.

There are two ways in which pain can be "soothed" within the organisation. The organisation can look at itself, work out what its pain is, and then go out to the market shopping for a solution. Alternatively, someone can approach the organisation looking to see if you have XYZ pain because, as if by magic, they have a solution for it.

Again from the supplier's perspective, this latter concept is horribly expensive for them. Practically when selling IT solutions into businesses, the only way that still works is some form of direct marketing: telemarketing, email marketing, LinkedIn direct messaging, mailshots, etc. Practically, organisations have got very good at rebuffing these sorts of marketing approaches. "Gatekeepers" that protect sales calls from reaching decision makers are now almost impregnable. Email marketing does work, but we see gradually declining open rates and other metrics over time. LinkedIn direct messaging is horrible now. Physical mailshots, peculiarly, aren't too bad because they have some novelty to them, but they are expensive. Because of this declining success around "cold outreach" methods, most sales and marketing effort is concentrated now and is about being visible when the organisation is out seeking a supplier to match its perceived pain.

In the business-to-business buying process, there is a loop that goes through various stages such as "unconscious dissatisfaction" (something is wrong, but they don't know what), "conscious dissatisfaction" (something is wrong, but they do know what), "recognition of needs" (they know the "shape" of a solution to fix the problem), "evaluating options" (finding out what in the market suits), "resolution of concerns" (building a business case, aligning vendor capabilities, risk control), and finally "decision/ contract". Only one of those stages – "evaluating options" – does the supplier's sales function get involved. In all the previous stages of that cycle, as far as the customer is concerned, the supplier is either (a) not important or (b) annoying.

What we find now is in the complex IT system sales, the supplier will look to position themselves as a "thought leader" and this will express itself through the expedient of providing free content to the market. Content such as blog posts, LinkedIn articles, videos, webinars, seminars and events, ebooks, books, all of this being positioned to educate you, the customer, about the pain that you may be having. When you start to go "oh wait, I have this pain in my organisation ..." the thought leader is already there and would be more than happy to have a conversation with you about it. In fairness, suppliers that are genuinely good at positioning themselves are experts do tend to have a genuine passion and aptitude for their particular specialism.

Having scores of business putting out constant streams of useful content about business and your potential issues is great news, but it depends on you and the organisation being able to identify the pain. (You're not missing anything by ignoring those sales calls or the 1.2 billion direct messages you get on LinkedIn every day.) Like the real world analogy this is supposed to align with, it's going to be better for your organisation to know about pain and deal with it when it's a small annoyance, as opposed to being the equivalent of your leg falling off that needs emergency treatment. That means you need to get better at strategy.

"What's So Special about You?" – The Seeds of Strategy

Ultimately, something has to stimulate the organisation into identifying a need for a new IT system, and if we continue to stretch our quasi-medical analogy from before there is a similarity between needing "emergency surgery" and "elective surgery". As was once explained to me by one particular doctor I was dealing with, "elective survey means you choose *when* to have it, not *if*" – the logic applies here too. It is much better to choose when your organisation engages with the market to procure a new IT system, rather than having the need to do so imposed upon you by external factors.

What we're ideally trying to do is defend against external factors impinging on us, but even with the best will (i.e. the best strategy) in the world, there is always a risk that some of them will force you to act before you ideally want to. A classic example of this are regulatory changes. For example, in the UK recently, HMRC (the UK's tax authority) rolled out a new regime called "Making Tax Digital", the idea being that organisations would have to submit tax documentation electronically. If you happened to be using a system within your organisation that did not support Making Tax Digital, you would have to upgrade or replace it. Another issue is that sometimes vendors will stop supporting a piece of software, and again you have to upgrade and replace it. Sometimes suppliers will rejig their pricing and turn a cost-effective solution into a "too expensive" solution, again meaning that you have to upgrade or replace it. All of these "have to" factors can push you into a corner, and it can all be very disappointing as you've already been through the process of getting the system deployed only to have to do that work again.

A particular risk point is that something external is setting the timescales for you, whereas ideally you want to set your own timescales. As we'll see when we go through the book, slippage in terms of time from the supplier is always a risk and something you have to proactively manage. But if there happens to be some external factor that's applying pressure as well, that again just lends credibility to the idea that you have to be more in control rather than less in control. For example, imagine facing the Making Tax Digital issue above, but at the same time the vendor has a compatible version that you can upgrade onto, but the cost of the new system is double what you were paying before. Now you have a very complex scenario to manage as you have to shift to a fresh vendor (that you likely have not dealt with before), within the timescale of the regulatory change, in addition to finding the money to do any of this. Complexity isn't a problem *per se*, but what can happen is that the organisation goes into a complex situation with its eyes closed and doesn't see problems that perhaps it should have done or could have done.

On the flip side of being made to buy an IT system is the option of choosing to buy an IT system. Here, though one of the issues that comes up is that the business is unable to evaluate its own needs and either (a) knows it needs to buy something, but doesn't know what or (b) doesn't know that it is supposed to buy something, let alone knows what. In these sorts of organisations, IT systems change can always feel like it is being "foisted upon" the business, rather than it being a more expressive and natural way of operating the business. Where we see this happen is where the business either does not have someone with IT strategy skills in-house. With someone competent overseeing the IT strategy, nasty surprises and blind alleys should be avoidable.

As businesses grow, we tend to see commonalities in how their IT capability matures, that is, there are common trends of growth. If you imagine any microbusiness with one or two employees, they will almost certainly have no IT function. Now imagine any global corporate with 100,000 staff, they almost certainly have an enormous IT function. At some point in the growth of any organisation, you reach an inflexion point where an IT function of some sort is introduced. Commonly this is achieved through outsourcing the IT to an IT support company. (This type of business is usually called a "managed service provider", or MSP.) However as the business grows, it will start to invest in its C-suite. Roles related to finance, operations, and sales/marketing will tend to emerge first. A decent-sized business can therefore have a CEO, CFO, COO, and CMO along with an outsourced IT function, but note a specific role related to IT is missing. Oversight of the IT needs of the business commonly ends up resting with the CFO; however, that person will almost certainly not be an IT specialist.

Strategy is most easily defined by an IT specialist – this makes sense as C-suite roles are strategic role. The discussion here is going to look at how you can start to do strategy even though this role is missing, although I will set out the trajectory of how organisations commonly embed proper IT strategy.

The C-suite role that the organisation needs in order to get an IT specialist on staff is either a Chief Information Officer (CIO) or a Chief Technology Officer (CTO). (This distinction is often confused, but I'll explain what each does as we go.) Practically, in the size of business we are talking about here, the distinction is rather artificial as you would be looking to hire someone who can flex between CIO and CTO as this sort of business won't have the budget for both. Broadly, CIOs look at internal IT use – that is, the IT systems the organisation operates in order to deliver whatever the organisation does. CTOs look outwards at how IT can improve the proposition to customers and partners. For example, a CIO may look to roll out a new accounting system. A CTO may look to roll out an app that lets a customer see the balance outstanding on their account.

Any C-suite hire is an expensive hire, so it is not unusual for businesses of this size to address the need on a part-time basis. There is some appetite within the industry to call this type of role "Fractional", that is, "Fractional CIO" or "Fractional CTO". I don't like this term at all, I prefer "consulting", but it boils down to the same thing. (I also did a quick survey on my LinkedIn when writing this and confirmed that virtually no one outside of the IT industry has heard the term.) However, this sort of consulting CIO/CTO role can be very powerful in getting competent IT strategy and leadership into the organisation.

As a side note, try not to rely on your IT support provider doing strategy work for you, unless you know that they are specifically good at it, and you are specifically paying them to do it. It may seem counterintuitive, but the majority of successful IT support businesses are founded by salespeople, not technologists. (There is a lot of margin to be made in provision of IT support services, and as alluded to above, selling IT support services is hard.) These businesses specialise more in "mechanical"-type IT operations and tend to "flit in and out" of the organisation rather than get fully invested to the point where decent strategy insights come to the surface. That said, some can be good – your mileage may vary.

To round that off then, it is likely if you're reading this that your business does not have a specific IT strategy skill, that the IT function is managed by someone who's primary skill set is not in IT, and so you have to "synthesise" your IT strategy using what you happen to have. Remember as well that using a consultant/fractional CIO/CTO can help.

Conceptualising Strategy

In these pages, I'm going to assume that the organisation doesn't have a problem with strategy generally, but it could benefit from some help on strategy around IT. To frame this, I'm going to set out that strategy is the work that we do to decide where we want to go in the medium and/or long terms, and we deploy tactics to drive the organisation along to achieve whatever strategic objectives we have set for ourselves.

The problem with building strategy around IT for a business that has no IT skills is that it is a minefield of "you don't know what you don't know". It is possible to build some elements of a strategy from first principles. Most businesses will have common objectives aligned with non-controversial, generally pleasing outcomes, for example: "increase margin", "grow the customer base", "reduce customer churn", and "improve cash flow". Organisations of all types often now have softer objectives either broadly around corporate social responsibility or employee wellbeing, etc.

Let's look at a worked example. We'll say the organisation has an objective (this being an element of strategy, not a strategy itself) of improving cashflow. One way to improve cashflow is to have better control over your debtors (people who owe you money). Reporting against your accounting system will show you this, and staff can use that report to send emails or make phones calls, and over time might turn an average payment time of, say, 45 days down to 30 days. (You can set whatever metrics you like.) Congrats, you have now achieved some progress against this strategic objective.

If I were looking at this problem for a real customer, I would not be talking about approaches to "improve cashflow", I would be describing the approach as "reducing friction on cash inflows". This is (a) more specific in terms of the direction of the flow of cash and (b) "friction" is at the time of writing a reasonably fashionable term for technical solutions that "get out of the way and make things happen". Again in a real customer, I'd be proposing two things – firstly, that the business looks a way to automate emails chasing payments to debtors, and, secondly, looking at solutions that directly reduced payment friction, in this case, direct debit solutions ("automatic payments" in the USA) from a vendor like GoCardless, or payment card solutions from a vendor like Stripe. (One of the first solutions are the emails, you can actually use some basic tools to make these emails look like they come from a real person in the accounts team, rather than an obviously automated email.)

I said about that this work would be an "objective" within a broader IT strategy. To tie that point up, the strategy would be quite broad: "use IT to improve operational efficiencies"; an objective within that strategy is to work to "reduce friction around cash inflows".

The only difference in the work that I am doing there as an IT specialist setting strategic objectives as compared to a non-IT specialist is that I know about the solutions that are on the market that can do this and know how effective (or not) they are when deployed. Much as I hate to show people behind the curtain and admit there's nothing special about my speciality, because we all have so much day-to-day interaction with computer systems (including carrying around supercomputers in our pockets able to retrieve all of human knowledge within seconds), we all tend to know these sorts of solutions exist even if it's not automatic to contextualise them within the organisations that we manage. In Starbucks just this week, the person behind the till/register asked me if I was going to pay with cash and I took me a while to work out why the question sounded odd. Is that such a leap to wonder why we're still relying on reconciling bank statements to see if customers have made payment as opposed to having other new-fangled solution to take money.

What we need to do though is turn happenstance into something more deliberate. In an organisation where there isn't an "IT thought leader" working day-to-day within the business, you have to create a sort of "crowdsourcing" solution to strategic IT problems. You need to get both better at identifying pain points, and better at understanding what solutions the market offers to that pain.

There are broadly speaking three different families of IT problems, and they are tiered in terms of cost and complexity. There are "commodity solutions" that everyone uses. The classic examples of these are Microsoft 365 and Google Workspace. Everyone uses one of these, and you should too. IT is now so prevalent within business that there are whole families of problems you no longer have to think about – you should just copy what everyone else does. The baseline of what everyone else does is what you should be doing. Don't do less than that baseline, and spend money on fixing this if you are not doing what everyone else does.

The second family of IT problems are looking to put your own slant on problems that everyone else has. The cashflow example above is an example of this sort of problem. Every business needs to manage debtors, and every business benefits from making it easier to bring cash in. If you can find a way of making some investment in IT that repays itself in term of real-terms efficiency gains (which you can read as "making it easier to get to where you need to get to"), then go right ahead.

The third family of IT problems are looking at optimising the one thing in your business that no one else does. In order to have a successful business, there will be some aspect of your offering to customers that is yours and yours alone. Marketeers call this a "unique selling proposition" (USP), but from a business strategy point of view this is a tool used to help business hone their marketing messages. Marketing aside, there will be a "secret sauce" within your business, which is the expression of the thing that you do better than anyone else. For example, you may produce the most efficient electric motor for use in electric vehicles, and your competitors may spend half their lives trying to work out how you sell that product for less than they sell something that's not as good. Or, you may be able to design an items of women's fashion and get into the shops faster than anyone else. Whatever it is, there will be a "moat" around your business that the business will naturally defend. (For example, Google has an enormous moat around search. Netflix used to have an enormous moat around video streaming, but now we see Disney, HBO, and others chipping away at that.) It's this third family of IT problems that you should concentrate the most attention on, because when you get good at this, you can make the business really excel.

If you're asking me to be more specific about how much attention, I would break it down that you should pay almost zero attention to the first family of issues that everyone has (email, file storage, telecommunications, and accounting), 50% of your effort on the second problem (optimising the things that you and your competitors all need to do, e.g. HR, training, CRM), and 50% of your effort on whatever your "moat" – that 50% should include data collection and analytics, and systems integration, alongside primary investment in systems to support your core "mission".

What you are looking to do from a strategic point of view is do a little work around culture change in that you need to everyone in the organisation looking for opportunities where IT systems modification may be of benefit. Obviously, what you likely have is a collection of people who are not IT specialists, and so you need to teach them to detect the "smell" of things within the organisation that could in theory be improved through the application of IT. (Once you make these detections, in the upper tiers of the organisation you then have to get better at the actual implementation part, but I'm assuming if you're reading this book you are ready to do at least one implementation.) The easiest way to do this is to

"train" the organisation to abhor manual processes.
Computers became popular in business because they allowed
automation and systematisation of manual processes, but we
still see businesses that are full of manual processes. You can
go a long way by just expunging all manual processes out of
the business. Even if you are finding arguments against the
direct value of doing this, there is always indirect value in
being able to release a staff member from spending a per-
centage of their week doing some rote manual task and giving
them the opportunity to use that released time to make more
creative input.

The second thing to look for is data. Data is becomingly
increasing important in business, and it is generally beneficial
to get the organisation better at dealing with data. You have
undoubtedly heard about this idea of a "revolution in artificial
intelligence". Much as it looks magical, artificial intelligence is –
at its core – applied statistics. It requires data to work, and as
such the best way to position your organisation to take
advantage of artificial intelligence tools as the cost comes down
and they become increasingly available is simply to "get good
at data".

In both of these instances, the change you want to lead your
organisation down is one where everyone in the business is
looking for and is open to the discovery of possibilities. You
don't need to be experts (yet) if you have a culture where
people are encouraged to (a) look for manual processes that
could be turned into automated or semi-automated processes,
and (b) look for places where data can be gathered and refined
for later processing. From there, it's then just a matter of listening to and learning as much as you can about how partner
organisations, your customers, and your peers get better at
working with working with IT systems and data. It also helps if
you learn and observe as much as possible how your life is
affected by the IT systems and data that you come across in
your everyday life.

What's in Your Basket?

At this point, we've managed to get about 10% of the way through this book without talking about what it is that you are actually buying, apart from setting out in the last chapter that we are primarily looking to purchase software, and that any hardware that we may buy is incidental to the core value delivered through software. Hold that thought, as we'll unpack a bit more specifics on market structure.

Back in the day, when computers were first becoming mainstream within business, it was fairly common to find that when someone needed some computer system to do something, someone would sit down and write a piece of software just to support that business. For example, if you ran a garage for repairing cars (an "auto repair shop" in the USA), you might go to someone who would write you a piece of software to support that particular business. If the software worked, the company that wrote the software might "genericise it" (make it less specific to the original business) and sell it as a software package.

This ended up being called "off-the-shelf" software, which for some reason gets lost to history then gets elongated to "commercial off-the-shelf software" and is usually given just the acronym "COTS". (Way back in the day there was a need to distinguish software for business/commercial use and personal use, but nowadays virtually the entire market for "personal off-the-shelf software" has been subsumed into apps that we install on our phones.) We will be talking a *lot* about COTS in this book – this book is effectively just about COTS software.

In the USA, the term "bespoke software" is relatively unusual, but I will use it in this book reasonably heavily because the alternative – "custom software" – will become ambiguous. Bespoke software is used to describe *fully featured* software applications that are written specifically for the organisation commissioning someone to write it, as opposed to the process of customising COTS software.

Over time, the industry has split so that now bespoke software is quite an unusual phenomenon. Most applications that are deployed into organisations today are COTS "packages" – that is, pieces of software, often very complicated pieces of software, that are configured such that they are (a) available to the users/staff within the business and (b) tweaked and "augmented" to suit the needs of the business. This tweaking and augmentation process is known as "customisation".

If you're reading this book because you have a specific IT project in mind, you are almost certainly looking to buy a commercial off-the-shelf software package and have it customised to suit your business. The core lesson of this book is (a) make sure you buy the correct base COTS package and (b) make sure that the customisations suit your needs.

Linking this back to our discussion earlier about "where should you put your effort" when implementing an IT system, if you recall we spoke about three types: (1) commodity solutions that everyone has, (2) solutions that are about incremental improvements to your business but that may not vary between you and competitors, and (3) solutions that are about core mission delivery, aka making your "moat" deeper and wider. When it comes to the first one – commodity solutions – the idea here is to buy the right commodity COTS package and *ideally* do very little customisation to it. The effort around customisation should go into the non-commodity solutions.

The reason for this is that implementation costs of IT solutions are eye-wateringly, staggeringly expensive. It is not unusual to see day rates for implementation that are £1,200 per day ($1,440 per day), and implementation does not take "one day". Even a simple six-week project at that sort of day rate will not give much change from £55k (£66k). And that is just the direct cost. Indirect costs such as slippage, having to redo work, or incidents that cause problems with one's career trajectory, business revenue and profits can all impact.

For example, Microsoft 365 and/or Google Workspace typically do not require much in the way of customisation to make them functional within the organisation, but they are still COTS packages. An enterprise resource planning (ERP) application such as SAP Business One or Microsoft Dynamics also are COTS packages, but require huge amount of customisation to make it functional within the organisation.

Interestingly though, although true bespoke software is quite unusual to find these days, the customisation that will have to be done in order to deliver your solution is technically "bespoke software". However, the distinction is perhaps unimportant. What you are buying is an off-the-shelf software package, and then customisation (which may include someone sitting down and writing specific software just for you) is part of the implementation. But we're nearing the end of this chapter, and in the next chapter we're really going to get into the teeth of that. We have a specific chapter on bespoke software coming up in Chapter 8.

Before we do though, I need to quickly cover off "the cloud".

The Cloud

Discussions about the cloud are unavoidable these days, and whatever solution you buy will likely involve the cloud, and also will almost certainly involve its evil stepsibling, "subscription payments".

There is a neat joke in IT circles which is this: "the cloud is just someone else's computer". What this means is that although what the cloud actually is can be somewhat ephemeral, all that happens with the cloud is that there is a bunch of computers somewhere connected to the internet that rather than you physically having to own, you connect to through the internet. The actual nature of these computers is no different to your laptop or desktop computer (practically, at least). The reason why we call it "the cloud" is because back when we in the IT industry used to draw diagrams of how things connected together, when we wanted to draw "the internet", we would draw a cloud, notionally because what was going on in there was (a) too complicated and (b) the details didn't matter.

The reason why cloud systems exist is partly because it benefits you and partly because it benefits the vendor.

When you have a computer (usually thought of as a "server") that you own and operate yourself, we call this "on premises", that is, "it's actually physically installed on your premises". The issue with computers that are on premises is that they can go wrong. They are also expensive to buy. When you stick, what is effect exactly the same computer, in a data centre there are certain ways that they can be managed where reliability issues go away. Also, computers are expensive to buy up-front, but this leads to a major problem with cloud solutions, which is that the industry loves "rent seeking".

Nowadays, the modern solution is that no one buys computers, but rather rents computer time from large-scale cloud providers – and by "no one", I mean not just you, but the software vendor who develops your COTS package also does this. A vast amount of software these days is sold on a "software as a service" or "SaaS" basis. What this does is transform the purchasing model from a high-cost capital expense (aka "capex") approach to a different approach which is based on operational expenses (aka "opex"). Note how I did not describe "opex" as "low-cost", but I did use the term "high-cost" in relation to the capex model.

A major reason why this is done from the vendor's perspective is that in a capex model, it's difficult to manage your cashflow. If you sell £10 m worth of product in a year on a capex basis, you might get paid all that cash in one quarter, and then be desperately running around trying to bring in cash for the next nine months. For example, you might sell 100 systems at £100k each, but happenstance means they all land in one quarter. (Or, there might be a global recession and suddenly everyone pauses their projects for six months.) In an opex model, every customer is paying you on a subscription, which might net you the same £10 m in sales, but now you know you're making ~£833k a month. Moreover, it takes a long time for that cashflow from customers' monthly spending to dry up, even if things are going badly for the business.

The problem for you as a customer is that it used to be possible to buy a solution on year for, say, £250k and then amortise the cost over a number of years. Yes, you'd have to raise the cash, but then the solution was yours. If you wanted to eke out the value from that £250k investment over 15 years, you could at least try, even if the system was only designed to last for 10 years. Personally, it's the "rent seeking" nature of this approach that I am not keen on. IT systems should be like any other form of plant or machinery that can be purchased by the organisation and be sat on the balance sheet as an asset. Organisations today are being shoved into a position where this essential "equipment" has to effectively be leased as continual operating expenditure.

Practically, as of the time of writing what you are likely looking at is a blend of approaches. Many systems are still sold on a "perpetual license" basis, meaning that you have a big capex cost for the software licenses, and then run on cloud servers that are charged on a monthly subscription/opex basis. It's "tradition" to charge annual maintenance charges to perpetually licensed software, and/or to see annual charges for access to helpdesk support. It will likely be quite rare that you have hardware costs to contend with, but we will go through this as we work through the examples. Implementation has been and will always be an up-front capex charge, this is the £1,200/$1,400 per day charge that I mentioned before. Because the industry does love this rent seeking approach (because of the benefit to cashflow, primarily) depending on what the shelf-life of this book turns out to be, you may find that the solution you're buying doesn't have perpetual licensing.

Summary

If you're a non-technical manager leading a project to purchase a new IT system, it's important to understand the broader context of information technology strategy. Human decision-making, both in business and personal contexts, is driven by emotions and rational justifications. When it comes to purchasing decisions, we often make emotional choices and then validate them using rational criteria. In the business-to-business purchasing process, decisions need to be justified with a solid business case. Overall, this chapter sets the stage for understanding the process of buying IT systems, the emotional and rational aspects of decision-making, and the importance of IT strategy within an organisation. As we head into the next chapter, we'll start to learn how we can clearly define what the organisation wants to build.

Chapter 2

Functional Specifications

In this chapter, we are going to look at functional specifications. These are easily the most important part of your new IT system from the perspective that if you get this part wrong, you can do the most damage. However, they are quite difficult to produce, especially for people who would describe themselves as "not technical". If you have a good functional specification, everything else that can go wrong in the project is considerably more manageable. If you have a poor functional specification, the project is pretty much doomed from the start. The functional specification informs everything – from the price, to the choice of solution, to the vendor selection, and to the day-to-day project management.

What Can Go Wrong with an IT Project?

Here's a quick précis of what can go wrong in an IT project. I have divided these into four groups, but interestingly by far the largest group of problems relates directly to the capability and involvement of the sponsoring organisation (i.e. you), *not* the supplier.

DOI: 10.4324/9781003427766-2

This first family of problems relates to **issues with the customer**. Primary amongst these are a **lack of clear goals and objectives** – that is, the organisation not being able to set out for itself the "why" behind the project. "Project" is sort of a poor term for what it is you are trying to do – it can be more properly described as a "mission", because this word conveys the importance of there needing to be a sense of clear leadership behind the project. This cuts two ways, because in order for there to be a leader, there needs to be something to lead. Therefore, this issue goes straight into issues around **lack of stakeholder engagement**, **lack of accountability**, **lack of internal resources** (i.e. principals within the organisation not believing in and supporting the project), and **lack of user involvement** (i.e. the people who will use the system not being particular bothered about it). Lack of user involvement goes directly to **insufficient training** – this being a factor that can ultimately kill a project even if everything else works. If the organisation does not believe in the project, you can run into issues with their being **insufficient budget**. Problems with leadership (e.g. the leadership being overbearing) can lead to issues around **unrealistic expectations**, especially if **political and cultural issues** prevent the organisation from being able to heal these sorts of issues. Sometimes the culture of the business is such that it is **unable to adapt** to the change that comes from the new system.

The second family of problems relates to issues with **project governance**. The biggest factor in this is **poor project management**. We will be looking this factor in much more detail in Chapter 6, but suffice to say for now that a major risk is allowing the vendor to do either (a) all the project management without your oversight, or (b) them not having any project management capability. Poor project management is often related to generally **poor communication**, especially if any or all of the issues in the family of problems described above are a factor. The reasons why "project governance" is broader than just "project management" is because of the importance of risk management – **inadequate risk management** is another major factor in project governance. Finally, whilst any project will vary its scope as it progresses towards completion, you are trying to avoid **uncontrolled scope creep** and temper that into "controlled variations in scope".

The third family of problems relates to the vendor. Sometimes you can just choose badly and end up making a **poor vendor selection**. This can be because the vendor never was able to do the work you have commissioned them to do. (For example, they may decide it's commercially expedient to offer a certain solution, but have no skills internally to deliver it.) Sometimes it's because they ordinarily would be able to, but something goes wrong and they can't. (Sometimes vendors go bankrupt mid-project – I worry about this frequently, and in my opinion more people should.) However, the internal operations of the vendor is both (a) opaque, and (b) outside of your direct control. As such, it's down to you to manage what you can – that is, the factors related to your own conduct as customer.

The final family of problems is related to the vendor in that **testing is inadequate**, or **quality control is inadequate**. The testing process we'll go over in detail in Chapter 10, but largely it's about creating an environment where the work is being checked and double-checked by both parties to make sure everyone is happy.

You will note from the above list that the first family of issues are the ones that are within your control – I like to say that these are "within your bailiwick" – and that they are all mostly soft skills, i.e. they don't require you or your colleagues to be fantastic tech-nologists. They are about creating space for the project within the organisation, and about applying sufficient leadership to deliver the project. It's going to help if you either already have a culture to support complex project delivery, or if you can meaningfully change that culture as you go. The second family of issues can be within your control, but these should be given to the vendor to do. Essentially, you are looking after the **culture**, they are looking after the **governance**. Things will go best if whilst you are looking after your culture, you are keeping an eye on their governance. Similarly, things will go best for them if they are looking after the governance and keeping an eye on your culture.

The third family of issues related to vendor selection is down to you. The clear approach here is to work with potential vendors as if they are operating from a position of good faith, but holding in mind the possibility that they are operating from a position of bad faith. We're going to look at vendor selection in Chapter 4. It's kind of like dating – you can assume the person you are talking to is nice, but there's a big difference between choosing someone to spend time with and choosing someone to marry. The work each of you are doing in each of those phases is different as well – once you are married, there is (should be) a clear plan as to how you are going to deliver the mission of that relationship.

The final family of issues we can leave for now and come back to, but essentially there are certain skills that come into play when it's time to actually get the new IT system operational within the business.

So then why is a functional specification important?

How Does a Functional Specification Make a Project Go More Smoothly?

Simply, the reason why a functional specification makes a project go more smoothly is that you have to know what it is you are trying to build. Specifically at this stage, *you* (as in the commissioning organisation) have to know what it is you are trying to build, and why, and be able to determine how much time and money it will cost.

It is very important to build out a "good enough" functional specification before you even start looking for a vendor. It's very tempting to allow a position where a vendor writes the specification for you. This is a situation that you should look to avoid, because although it's almost certain true to say that a competent vendor probably can write a "better" specification than you can if given the opportunity, going down this road gives the vendor more power than you would like them to have at this stage. We're going to go in this later, but essentially if you invite a vendor into your business so that they can write the specification, chances are they will end up winning the project outright as when interpersonal professional relationships between customer and vendor develop, that vendor will tend to win any work that's on offer. It's quite common for the customer to give up on the concept of competition entirely once a relationship with a partner gets sufficiently good.

In the last section we spoke about how two main ways to derail a project were (a) problems with you (the customer) and effectively a lack of commitment, and (b) project governance issues. A good functional specification will cover off risk associated with both of these families of problems.

A functional specification has to be "canonical", which in these pages I'm going to define as meaning "complete". Anything that the system can do that the business will rely on has to be set out somewhere within the specification. At the functional specification stage, if the solution is to be based on a COTS application, you may not know the product that you wish to deploy – for example, you may know that you want a ERP system, but you do not know if you are going to choose SAP Business One or Microsoft Dynamics at this point. (If you're unfamiliar with these packages, I mention them just for illustration purposes – the specifics of the implementation is not important.) You should write the specification in a way that is "agnostic" to the specific package that you may end up rolling out. For example, if you are trying to describe in the specification that pallets received into a warehouse have a barcode that needs to be scanned, you can just talk about this without needing to talk about how SAP Business One *as a specific package* deals with receipt of goods. (We'll look at how you actually write a specification in a moment.) Indeed, it can be helpful to take this approach as it avoids being "tunnel-visioned" into how a specific package performs a function that you want to include and lets you write authentically from a position setting out the needs of the business as opposed to writing from a position informed by the capabilities of the software that you are looking to implement.

Like all things in life, writing specifications gets easier with practice, and its for this reason that a vendor is likely going to write a "better" specification than you – they've had more chance to practice. In addition, most people find writing specifications to be a fairly boring process. It takes a certain type of personality to be able to write a specification, and you may need to operate the process within your business such that the person or people writing the specifications are well-suited to the task. What you're looking to achieve with a specification is effectively creating a list of the rules within the business that govern your operations, as they pertain to any computer system that support those operations. As I said before, this list has to be canonical – this effectively means that every rule has to be detailed. (And every subrule has to be detailed too.) Don't, therefore, give the job of writing the specification to someone who isn't a fan of dotting every "i" and crossing every "t". Not to stereotype, but if you happen to have a senior finance person who can't sleep at night if an expense claim is missing a receipt, they may be well-suited to writing a specification.

"MUST" and "COULD"

The biggest error that people make when writing specifications is not giving them enough structure or enough of a formal tone. If you recall in Chapter 0, I added a diagram that showed the process of structured decomposition from the concept of what a system needed to do down to the lines of code that was the actual implementation of the software. Here's that diagram again:

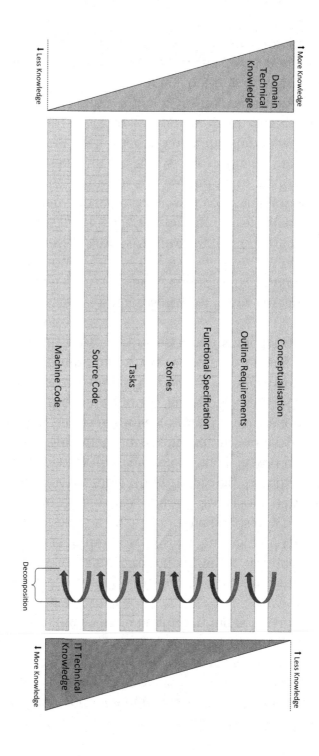

It's unlikely that as someone reading this book you will have hands on experience at writing software code – and it's of course perfectly fine that you do not. Software code is very different to writing in plain English (or any other language) because it specifically looks to remove ambiguity. There is no such thing as "inferred meaning" when you are writing software – it's a very "black and white" process.

If you were describing to someone how to print an invoice, you might say to them: "Press that button, and the invoice will print". The person then presses the button, and (probably) the invoice will print. The engineer in me needs to write "probably" in there because there are a bunch of reasons why the invoice won't print. For example, the printer may be offline, or it may be out of paper. Or the customer details linked to the invoice might be missing an address, and when you try to print it out the code that builds the invoice might crash as a result. In the user's world, the thing should "just work", but in the engineer's world, there are hundreds of reasons why it won't work. Of course, the printing might work. From an engineer's perspective, it's usually more surprising when something works then when it does not.

What you can't do when software is just say, in plain language, "Take the invoice, and send it to the printer", because it is too ambiguous.

We have a very simple example here, and you may be thinking at this point that that example doesn't give scope for *too* much ambiguity. Imagine if you will receiving goods into a warehouse. The shipment arrives, and you scan the barcode on the pallet, checking in the goods. Great. But the next month you need to place a larger order and now the shipment comes in two pallets. Can you check in a shipment that has two barcodes for two pallets? What is the shipment is three pallets and number two is missing? What if it's two pallets, but number one is missing? What if it's four pallets, and three arrive today and the final one has been sent on a lorry tha won't be here until tomorrow? What if someone rips off the barcode by accident? What if someone steals the barcode scanner? What if power goes out to the building when you're checking in a two-pallet order and you've scanned in one pallet and not the other one? An engineer will think of all of this, but someone who is not an IT specialist specifying a system probably won't.

As we go down through the layers, we know that the top layer that states the overall system concept is very vague and has a lot of ambiguity. We also know that the bottom layer that is the actual software code is very precise and has zero ambiguity. As we progress down the layers, ambiguity is expunged. We do, however, have choice as to how much ambiguity we remove at each layer. As everything apart from the bottom software layer is written in plain language, we always have some inherent ambiguity in these layers by virtue of the fact that they are expressed in plain language. What newcomers to writing specifications tend to do is that they allow too much ambiguity to persist in the higher layers.

The trick to avoid this is to try and make the specification less prosaic and more expressive. However, I mean "expressive" as it's meant in computer science circles – I'm not implying that you sit down and bash out 10,000 words in iambic pentameter about how the light coming from the east is the beauty of your credit control report. What you're actually looking to do is be far more "declarative" in how you write. You're looking for something closer to a recipe as opposed to a narrative description. There is a trick you can use to help make this transition, which I'll set out in a moment.

Consider first though this description:

```
Receiving goods into a warehouse is a crit-
ical process that involves the physical
receipt of items from suppliers or manufac-
turers into the warehouse inventory system.
```

The process starts with the arrival of the goods at the warehouse loading dock. The warehouse personnel are responsible for inspecting and verifying the received items' quantity, quality, and condition against the purchase order or invoice.

Upon arrival, the goods are usually unloaded from the supplier's delivery truck, and the receiving team uses equipment such as pump trucks or forklifts to transport the items into the warehouse. The team then matches the received items with the corresponding purchase orders or invoices, checking for any discrepancies such as damaged or missing items.

Once the items have been verified, the team updates the warehouse inventory system, indicating that the goods have been received and are ready for storage.

Those 168 words describes the process of receiving goods into a warehouse. Of those three paragraphs, two of them have an impact on any computer system that may support this operation – we need to be able to track corresponding purchase orders, we need to be able to flag damaged or missing items, and we need to indicate receipt into the warehouse.

It would not be unusual to find a description like this in a functional specification, but it's lack of declarative factors leads us reading between the lines to an "overmuch" degree. The first job is to re-draft the specification reducing the amount of "reading between the lines" that is required.

However, there's nothing wrong with putting narrative descriptions in a functional specification if it supports the reader in understanding the business operation, especially if the business operation is unfamiliar to the reader. Ideally, every person in the organisation is a potential audience member for the functional specification, so it's important to add colour and try and bring the specification to life as much as you can. Also remember that any vendor that you are courting to deliver this system will also need to read the specification. The *right level* of detail will help everyone out.

Finally, it is important that you tell a compelling story. Each part of the specification has to have a beginning, a middle, and an end. And your story has to have a protagonist – that protagonist being the user, and everything you write has to be written from the perspective of the user. Hopefully I'm not overstretching the analogy, but you are also looking to deliver a happy ending in that the story you tell needs to end with the user getting the results they want out of the system. (We will later learn that a key part of the delivery involves writing things that are literally called "user stories".)

Going back to our specific example, we could write more detail into the specification like this:

```
When the supplier's delivery truck arrives at
the warehouse, it will be expected. One of the
warehouse staff needs to be able to access a
screen where they can find the record of the
purchase order related to the shipment. That
purchase order will contain a list of items
that are supposedly in the order. Some of the
items might be missing, or might be broken or
otherwise unsuitable. The goods should be
loaded onto pallets that can be received into
the warehouse.
```

This is a fairly typical example of how a specification gets written, not just by non-technical "amateur" specification authors, but many professional service firms will write specifications like this as well. I'm going to give you a steer and strongly suggest that you use a different technique in writing your specifications based on a quite old (1997) technical standard called "RFC 2119: Key words for use in RFCs to Indicate Requirement Levels".

Specifically:

> The trick with RFC 2119 is to (a) avoid running on and linking statements, and (b) have at least one declarative key word per statement. Those key words can be one of MUST, MUST NOT, SHOULD, SHOULD NOT, and MAY, and where those words exist, you always put them in upper case. Other declarations that provide context must also be given in upper case, especially cardinal numbers.

… or to actually restate that in RFC 2119 style:

> Statements written in RFC 2119 style MUST NOT have conjoining statements.
>
> Statements MUST have at LEAST ONE OF the following declarative key words stating intent: MUST, MUST NOT, SHOULD, SHOULD NOT, or MAY.
>
> Where a key word is used, it MUST be written in UPPER CASE.
>
> Related declarations MUST also be given in upper case. Cardinal numbers are ONE example of related declarations.

If you contrast those two examples, they say the same thing, but in the second RFC 2119-compliant version, it is far easier to discern what the rules are because we break down each rule into its own sentence on its own line and state that it MUST be done. I am fairly sure that you, the reader, would find the second version easier to follow?

If we take that same approach with the narrative above, we get this:

When a delivery truck arrives at the warehouse, the shipment MUST have AT LEAST ONE purchase order recorded in the system.

The order SHOULD be packaged onto AT LEAST ONE palette, although the order MAY come otherwise packaged.

A warehouse staff user MUST be able to query the purchase order related to the shipment.

The purchase order display MUST contain a list of purchase order line items that are on the order.

EACH purchase order line number MUST contain (a) the description, (b) the supplier reference number, AND (c) the quantity ordered.

It MAY be the case that items on the order are missing. It MUST be possible for the user to record missing items.

It MAY be the case that items on the order are damaged. It MUST be possible for the user to record damaged items.

The user MUST be able to mark items that have been received as RECEIVED.

Again, we've taken an (admittedly shorter) narrative/proasic blurb and turned it into a more detailed set of rules, but the rules we've used to build the rules are not complicated and do ultimately produce something that is easier to understand because we have to do less reading between the lines to understand what is going on (i.e. it's easier to interpret). Reading that revised specification, we know we have purchase orders, that the user needs a screen by which to retrieve the purchase orders, and know that for each item they can either reject items because they are missing or damaged, or they can accept items. (If you're thinking there's more than this that can go wrong, we'll get to that.)

Personally, having spent my life in IT, I prefer to read specifications like that, however a major reason why we write them like that is because it's more aligned with the actual work that needs to be done. Ultimately, there has to be a screen that let's the user find purchase orders. We have the statement that says "*A warehouse staff user MUST be able to query the purchase order related to the shipment*". At some point in the process, someone has to build (or make available) that screen – having it written as a single line, without ambiguity, in the specification means it's far harder to omit it from the final delivery.

Preferring Exceptional Cases

There are two more things that we need cover off around specifications – exceptional cases, and completeness.

Throughout the earlier pages, I've sought to give you an overview as to how software is constructed, and in particular I spoke about how software looks to take known inputs and transform them to get known outputs. What I didn't tell you when I wrote that is that one of the reasons why writing software is hard is because it is almost impossible to know what inputs you will deal with when the user is using your software. Most of the effort that goes into writing software goes into defending against users inputting "bad" or "unexpected" data.

You can think of these as exceptional cases – that is, they are the "cases that are the exceptions to the rules".

By way of an example, if you've read everything up to this point, you have read about 14,000 words of bumpf that I have typed into Microsoft Word. No one has ever put those exact 14,000 words into Microsoft Word in that order before, yet it has not crashed once. The construction of the software is such that anything weird and exceptional that I may have done when writing the proceeding words was not so weird or exceptional so as to crash the software.

Your functional specification describes software, as such *you* have to deal with exceptional cases in your functional specification. To be honest, this is a very difficult skill in systems engineering to achieve, so my guidance here is seeking to nudge you in the right direction rather than transform you into someone who is good at it on their first try.

Within the system you can conceptualise a "good path" (i.e. the stuff you want to happen), and a whole mess of "bad paths". The more of the bad paths that get encapsulated in the specification at this stage the better. However, it will ultimately be the vendor's responsibility to do this as the more definition you have over the bad paths, the better the implementation will be. We'll talk more about ways in which conflicts between customer and vendor arise in Chapter 11, but omissions of "bad paths" in functional specifications is an important source of conflict.

In the specification above, we stated these two "bad paths":

```
It MAY be the case that items on the order are
missing. It MUST be possible for the user to
record missing items.
```

```
It MAY be the case that items on the order are
damaged. It MUST be possible for the user to
record damaged items.
```

There are more of them. For example:

It MAY be the case that FEWER items than were on the order are supplied. It MUST be possible for the user to accept fewer items, OR accept an ad hoc quantity, OR reject the line.

It MAY be the case that MORE items than were on the order are supplied. It MUST be possible for the user to accept MORE items, OR accept an ad hoc quantity, OR reject the line.

It MAY be the case that the user seeks reject ANY quantity UP TO AND INCLUDING ALL ITEMS of ANY line item. (For example, the warehouse manager may be asked to reject an item because of a safety issue that became apparent in the time between the order placed and the shipment arriving.)

... and even then there may be more. But you can see even in this simple example we have 14 words describing the "they sent us what they said they would" case (i.e. the good path), and 171 words describing the "bad path" cases. Note as well that the bad path cases are almost always more complex. To summarise though, this rule is that you should always *prefer exceptional cases*.

Aiming for Completeness

As mentioned above, it's critical that the specification that you produce is canonical – that is, it needs to encompass all of the functionality that the organisation needs the system to do. Another way to put this is that it needs to have proper breadth. (You can consider the point above about the specification seeking to prefer exceptional cases as being about the "depth".)

For this one, I can't give you any tricks or guidance other than "you'll know it when you see it". When you start the specification process, you will have your conceptual idea of the project in mind. This will give you some top-level items that you need to deliver, and this will tell you the people and processes involved. As you document the processes and interview and work with more people in the organisation, you will (hopefully/probably) end up documenting the entire system specification. A good thing to look at is the key performance indicators (KPI) that are related to the system performance. From knowing what these KPI and associated reporting measures are, you can likely backfill the areas that need specifying.

This is likely to be the first part where you genuinely need support of the partner to help deliver the specification as this is where you can leverage their consultative capabilities – they will have seen businesses like yours and projects like yours, which we'll go on to talk about now. However, I'll reiterate my earlier point before I do. It is very important not to give the partner too much power by asking them to do too much of the functional specification. If the partner uncovers areas of the system requirements that you within the organisation do not know like the back of your collective hands, you need to take this as a cue from the partner to make these determinations yourselves. To re-reiterate, do not rely on the partner to determine the needs of the business. Instead, you need to use them to *refine your understanding* of the needs of the business.

Formal Scoping and Pre-design

There is no reason in the world why a competent management team of a capable organisation cannot write a better-than-good-enough functional specification. However, most teams do not write functional specifications because they either (a) don't know they should, or (b) don't know how. Hopefully the preceding pages make you (and your team) feel confident that you can.

However, the thing that a non-technical team cannot do is come up with a price. For that, you now need to involve a partner, and by far the best way to do this is via a "scoping exercise". Although we're going to talking about scoping here, you will not actually commission a scope until you have been through the supplier selection, which we talk about in Chapter 4. For now, you just need to get your head around what a scoping exercise is, but please remember that the scoping exercise comes in later in the process.

As mentioned in Chapter 1, the cost of acquisition to a supplier of acquiring you as a customer is eyewatering. Part of the reason or this is that customers do not enter the market very often. You may need to update a core IT system once every ten years, and when you do that you're marketable-at, but if you have an IT system that works any marketing that comes your way is just going to be noise. Another part of the reason is that when you are in the market, the *cost of making a mistake* from the customer's perspective is sky-high, not just in real terms, but there can be reputation and career-affecting indirect costs. Ultimately, the supplier needs to bring the trust up and the risk down from the customer's perspective. This means the supplier has to be an expert, and in order to be an expert you – the customer – have to believe that they can deliver what you want.

The easiest way to do this, from the supplier's perspective, is to do something a little bit like psychotherapy. The customer has to tell the supplier what they want. The supplier then has to repeat back what they want, but in such a way that the customer is comfortable that the supplier "gets it". Again looping back to Chapter 1, the supplier has to demonstrate that they can soothe the customers' pain, whatever that pain happens to be. Like all good sales processes, this is nothing to do with the "features and benefits" of the product or service being sold in – it is 100% related to the customer's perception that whatever pain they are suffering with will go away.

The only proper forum in which to do that is via consultancy. The supplier has to have a lot of trusted access to you and the team in order to listen to what you want and then repeat back that they have understood it. This means you have to sit down in a room, be interviewed, and then a report has to be produced, which then has to be read and absorbed – that is, consultancy. In the scenario of IT systems procurement, this process is called a "scoping exercise", that is, a small scale consultancy exercise designed to formalise the needs that you as a customer have.

There is one "problem" with scoping exercises in that they are *incredibly* value to the supplier in reducing the cost of acquisition. However, whilst they are valuable to the supplier, they are of genuine value to the customer as well. It is helpful to have a trusted technical advisor check your work and make sure that what you are trying to implement is a good fit for your business. As such, there is a symbiotic balance between customer and supplier with regards to scoping exercises.

The danger with scoping exercises is that they can happen backwards. You as the customer *must* know what you want to build before you commission the scope. This is why this chapter is structured to (hopefully) make you feel confident and comfortable about producing a functional specification before you go into scoping. Any supplier that you will approach for a complex IT system will try and pitch you on a scope, and they will sell it to you on the basis of controlling your risk. Most customers when they enter the market will have a rough idea what they want to have delivered, but they don't tend to get further through the process than developing the rough idea. Rough ideas are risky – refined and thought-through ideas are less risky. The vendor will find it very easy to pitch you on the idea of quantifying risk at a much reduced cost. A scope will cost you 5%–10% of the estimated final project cost – so if you're looking at a £250k/$280k project a scope will cost you £12.5k-£25k/$14k-$28k.

As mentioned, a major problem with scoping is that once you have done one, if you are going to do the project, you almost certainly will choose the vendor who did the scope to deliver. As the price is 1/20th or 1/10th lower – and through pricing psychology now seems very cheap in comparison – the danger is that the organisation will choose a vendor through a poor or ineffective competition process. (You're not supposed to be finding someone good enough to deliver a £20k/$24k report, you're looking to drop a huge amount of money on a system you have to live with for a decade or more.)

What you want to do with a scoping exercise is have the supplier (a) check your work, (b) come up with some insights as to how to improve your first draft, and (c) come up with a *reliable* price estimate.

What a Scoping Exercise Does

We're going to talk about pricing more in the next chapter, but for now the basics of how to come up with a price for the solution is relatively easy as it is tied directly to effort. In the last chapter I gave some indicative pricing of £1,200/$1,400 per day. The easiest way to get a good estimate of the effort is to go through each feature referenced the specification in turn, estimate how long each one will take, and sum up the estimates. If the vendor is able to estimate the effort at 30 days, the price will simply be 30 days multiplied by the day rate.

On our example above of receiving goods into the warehouse, the way that we have written the specification makes it easier to identify the functions, and as such easier to go through and tot up the total. Just for illustration, it might take a half-day to implement the function to allow the purchase order(s) related to the shipment to be queried, a half-day to present it on the screen, a half-day to implement the "good path" of a successful receipt, and two days to deal with the identified "bad paths", giving a total of three-and-a-half days. Multiply that by the day rate to get the price.

It is not possible to come up with a good estimate without a good functional specification. As most customers do not know how or do not know they should produce their own functional specification, most scoping exercises look to synthesise the *only* functional specification as their primary output, with a cost estimate (i.e. a quote) as the secondary output. If you're taking the steer that I'm keen for you to take in these pages, if you do a scoping exercise you would already have produced a functional specification. It is up to you whether the one you produce forms the foundation of the work that the vendor does, or you seek to compare and contrast both specifications. This will be "chef's choice" depending on how you feel you can get the best value out of the spend with the vendor.

As I mentioned before, a scoping exercise will cost about 5% to 10% of the estimated cost of the project. (The vendor will have a sense as to how much the final project will cost, in much the same way that an experienced plumber visiting a house to install a new boiler will be able to "ballpark" the final figure just from the initial presentation.) A relatively small spend of that magnitude will hugely help to "de-risk" the project, and give you a sense as to whether you can work with the vendor on long-term. They are an essential part of the delivery process.

Summary

The success of your project starts and ends with the quality of your specification. Generally, if you have a good specification, you project can't fail. (Your mileage may vary!) The functional specification outlines what needs to be built, why, and the estimated time and cost involved.

A common error is letting the supplier write the specification. Whilst they are likely "better" at writing specifications, part of the specification authoring process is to allow the organisation the opportunity to learn what it is it is trying to do and why – the answer to both of these questions feed into the project itself, and it's through this mechanism that the chances of project success are increased.

A functional specification must be complete and canonical, covering all the system's necessary functions and rules. It should be written in a way that is independent of specific software packages, focusing on the business needs rather than software capabilities. Writing specifications requires attention to detail and a structured approach. We saw a method – which I'm very fond of – of how to write the language within specifications to make them more expressive and readable. The goal is to provide precise instructions for the system's functionalities, leaving no room (more realistically, "only little room") for interpretation or confusion.

Chapter 3

The Shape of
the Solution

Whether you're buying something personally or for business, in our Western late-stage capitalist approach to consuming, in principle it's supposed to be a rational, two-party transaction comprising an offer and subsequent acceptance. However, the way that this actually shakes out is that when we're buying things we're supposed to "stay in our lane" and not consider too much the machinations that are happening on the supplier's side. For example, I'm sitting in a Starbucks writing this and I'm pretty sure that the coffee I'm enjoying whilst I'm drinking it has a whopping profit margin built in, but I have no idea whether I've just handed over 20p in margin, or £2. If it were a properly rational, properly fair transaction, I would know exactly what contribution I was making to the supplier's profit.

Personally, I'm a great believer that there is a lot of power in giving the customer visibility into how supplier's work out their pricing and how much profit they make. As such, a big part of the value of this chapter is in letting you peek behind the curtain as to how the supplier is pricing their offer.

DOI: 10.4324/9781003427766-3

The Basics of IT Project Pricing

The overriding principle of pricing in delivery of IT systems projects is that the supplier is looking to make a profit. Whilst there are some volunteering and charitable organisations that support non-profits in IT systems delivery, these all operate on a very small scale. (In reality, large charitable organisations tend to be very lucrative for IT suppliers because they tend to be awash with cash.)

The reason why I bring this up first is because you should always be pushing suppliers for fixed price projects. Fixed price projects are effectively based on applied guesswork, but this is not a bad thing. The things that we've discussed thus far about developing really good specifications and having well-executed, tight scopes are designed to make the "guess" the supplier delivers with regards to pricing more accurate.

The problem with the guess being inaccurate is that although you would think that's the supplier's problem, it's not – an inaccurate guess ends up being *your* problem and is the Number 1 cause of (legal) disputes between customers and supplier.

Whatever solution you are buying, there is one thing that can be said for certain, and that is that the thing that you are buying is *fantastically* expensive. You are going to give the customer a sum of money, and expect the solution delivered. If the solution cannot be delivered for that sum of money, the supplier has to make up the difference, but because what you are buying is so expensive, in real terms that is very painful for the supplier. For example, if the price of the project is £250k/$300k, the supplier might want to make £50k/$60k profit – that is, they're taking your £250k/$300k and spending £200k/$240k. If their estimate is wrong – or something goes horribly wrong on the project and the project actually *costs* £350k/$420k, they are not only not making any profit, but they are actually having to reach into their pocket and start spending their own money delivering your solution.

Whilst this is an ethically-defensible position, the reason why this causes conflicts is that suppliers optimise their resource available in-line with their profit motives – that is, if a project is bleeding money, the supplier will tend to want to direct resources to other projects that are rich in profit. As such, in situations where a project is going badly, you can find that your supplier's team – that knows you and your organisation – may well evaporate as the supplier looks to preserve their overall profits. To put it another way, failing projects from the supplier's perspective tend to deteriorate and dribble along. This is counterintuitive compared to what you think would happen – that the supplier would put the best people on the project to get it cleared and out of the door as quickly as possible, however this sadly is not what happens. The best way to avoid conflicts (and to build a good relationship) is to ensure that the supplier can make a profit out of the project.

Of course, projects don't have to be delivered on a fixed-price basis, but it is substantially better if they are. There is another way that projects can be billed, which is on a time and materials basis. However, in most cases time and materials projects should be avoided. They are good for projects where a good estimate genuinely cannot be determined – and this realistically means that these are projects that are highly experimental in nature. The typical reader of this book should ideally not be looking to introduce an IT system that involves a high level of experimentation – if you want to do something like that, you should engage someone to bring IT strategy into the organisation and have them run the experiment. This can be done fairly easily by bringing in a fractional/consulting CIO or CTO into the business.

In summary then – you should always seek a fixed price project, and avoid time and materials projects, but it's critical to ensure that you work with the supplier to ensure that the project will realise a profit for them as "obliging" a supplier to work on an unprofitable project effectively guarantees one of two outcomes:

"conflict" as in "just an argument", or a "Conflict" as in "you're heading to court".

Determining Price

We've spoken at length about profitability for the supplier – the other part of the pricing piece is the cost.

The most profitable part of an IT supply engagement for the supplier is the professional services part, these days, anything a supplier buys in order to sell on to you attracts very low margins. For example, there is no margin to be made from IT hardware supply. If you are buying laptops, desktops, servers, or peripherals, unless you are buying in huge numbers, the prices you see at retail (e.g. at Amazon) are close to wholesale price from distribution. If a supplier is trying to sell you hardware, although they will make a little bit of money from it, the value that they are selling you is in selling a holistic solution. The supplier gets to have a say as to what you are buying, and can do some value-add work in making sure that what has been ordered will suit your needs, and if anything isn't going quite right they can liaise with the vendor on your behalf.

The reason why there is very little margin on IT hardware supplier is because hardware are commodity items, and commodity items always create a "race to the bottom" by obliging suppliers to compete primarily on price as opposed to on other value points. Commodities are standardised or interchangeable – you can walk into any office in any industry and see someone using a laptop, and it doesn't matter too much if it's a Dell, HP, Lenovo, or a MacBook.

When we look at software as opposed to hardware, we can apply this commoditisation principle to certain parts of the "software stack". Microsoft 365 comprises two sets of software modules – the productivity apps that (effectively) everyone needs to use, that is, Word, Excel, PowerPoint, and Excel, and cloud services. Those cloud services are Exchange for email, and SharePoint/OneDrive for file sharing (There are bunch of other services that are in Microsoft 365 too, but these two are the main ones). The biggest sell for Microsoft 365 in business is the hosted Exchange email service. Microsoft 365 has just one competitor in Google Workspace. A deep-dive on the pros and cons of either in your business is out-of-scope for this book, but what both of these products do is commoditise email delivery. (The Office apps are both commoditised and monopolised – every business needs these to the extent that they are simply a cost of doing business.) It is rare to find a business where email provision through either Microsoft 365 or Google Workspace is not the best solution. Turning this discussion round to think about commoditisation, what the existence of both of these solution does is to destroy the market for alternatives because they are a) an interchangeable, standard "component", and b) very cheap.

Someone reselling Microsoft 365 to your business is going to make 15% margin on that sale. In order to make more than they, they will have to be moving a *lot* of subscriptions. This means that on your £9.40/$12.50 (as of the time of writing) per user subscription, your reseller is making £1.40/$1.90. It's only interesting to sell Microsoft 365 if you are selling thousands-upon-thousands. As is the case when selling you hardware, wrapping Microsoft 365 into your solution is being done to provide a "holistic convenience" as opposed to creating a centre of profit.

Profit starts to come when we move into specialisation, either vertical specialisation (industry alignment), or horizontal specialisation (functional alignment). This happens because although there is competitive pressure, there is not the same degree of interchangeability that leads to commoditisation because over a certain scale any solution requires customisation. Regardless, where you have a high degree of specialisation, you also tend to see a sort of "informal protectionism" in that people playing in this space tend not to want to cannibalise their markets and margins by a price-based race to the bottom.

What vendors in specialised markets are trying to achieve is that they either want to sell either a) licenses and support, or b) subscriptions, but they want the implementation/consultancy work that is required to make the solution work for the customer. The balancing act comes in in that the actual valuation of the supplier's business is affected by how these are mixed. Valuations of businesses of this type are biased towards product sales as opposed to implementation fees, so in order to drive high valuations so that the owners can eventually see the trade sale exit they seek, they want to get this mix just right and build profitability through implementation but valuation through sales. This set-up effectively guarantees that from now until the end of time, complex IT systems (which by definition are specialised) will always be sold into you on an implementation/consultancy basis. Further, there are two ways this can be sold to you – either as a) perpetual licenses with support, or b) as monthly subscriptions.

Software traditionally was sold as perpetual licenses with support, and when sold in this mode buying software was analogous to buying plant or equipment. Any purchase made of this type came as a "capital expenditure", or "capex" and was expensive in real terms. Businesses had to amortise and account for this capital expenditure as they did with deprecation on plant or equipment. Support, whilst delivering genuine value, was hit upon as a wizard method to keep extracting spend from the client over the life of the system. Margins on this sort of spend sit at around 35%.

You may have noticed that so far in this book we have only mentioned "the cloud" very briefly, yet the idea of "the cloud" will be unavoidable to anyone trying to implement a complex IT solution. The reason for this is because of the old joke: "the cloud is just someone else's computer". There isn't anything magical or weird about the cloud. If a company is buying a cloud solution, it is exactly the same hardware and software configuration that you would buy for yourself, but packaged and delivered in a different way.

Back in the day, if you wanted to deploy a solution, you would need the following items at a minimum: the hardware, the software, a building to put it in, some physical security paraphernalia, an electricity supply, one or more connections to the internet/network, and one or more human beings to keep it running. Depending on how big and complex we are talking about, you may also need a cooling solution, a fire suppression solution, and/or backup power generators. Today, to differentiate from cloud deployments, we call this "on premises" solutions, which is often shortened to "on prem". The primary problem with on premises solution is that they attract a high capital cost. The secondary problem is that keeping an IT system up and running is difficult, and economies of scale kick in through consolidation.

Cloud computing is nothing more complicated than outsourcing. Rather than having to build your own datacentre that you put your own computers in, and have someone run it all, all of that work is outsourced to someone who already has a datacentre and a bunch of staff who want to keep all of the computers inside running. (You can think of "cloud computing" as "cloud hosting" as this is really all it is – someone is renting you servers and then hosting your solution on an outsourced basis.) The absolute genius part of a cloud computing approach is that the people selling them put a lot of effort into reducing "friction" around approval and payment of the solution. Now rather than having to explain to the board that you want to make a £500k/$600k capex to build a datacentre to run your solution, you just have to explain to the board that you are going to spend £10k/$12k per month as an "operational expense" (aka "opex").

You will, over the long-term, pay more for a cloud solution than an on-premise solution – if you ignore the "soft" advantages of the cloud. Generally, you will get better reliability and increased security through cloud deployment.

What people tend to forget to do when pricing up cloud solutions is they either forget to amortise the capex, or multiple up the opex to get an equal comparison. Over five years, our illustration above amortised out at £8.3k/$10k a month. It's absolutely critical to get an "apples to apples" comparison because what can happen is that you lose some of the due diligence. Organisations tend to go quite slow when making large capex payments but can more easily square away (even quite large) monthly opex payments. This can result in, even though the same amount of money is being spent overall in real terms, there is less stringent qualification in deals based on what is effectively this "outsourced" subscription model.

There is also one important risk point to consider when outsourcing in this way, and that how quickly a solution can get killed off when outsourced. If you own the solution end-to-end, there is a certain resilience that comes from ownership that you lose with outsourced solutions. For example, if you own the data centre and roadworks outside results in the fibre connection to the building being cut, you can ultimately fix that problem yourself, even if it involves chaining yourself to the railings outside the comms company until they send an engineer out to effect a solution. Similarly, even quite large solutions, if you physically own the equipment – there a few problems you can't solve with a weekend, a rental van, and a few friends. Simply load your kit into the back of your van, get it under your control, and get it somewhere where whatever is not working can be made to work. This is not the case with outsourcing/cloud solutions where you don't own anything. If your outsourced provider finds they don't have the money to pay the electricity bill (or the staff, or the equipment lease payments, or the any one of a hundred things that can go wrong), your system can get switched off and there is essentially nothing you can do about it. As an IT specialist that builds and runs complex IT systems every day, one thing that keeps me awake at night is supplier bankruptcy. This is a risk point that organisations simply do not think about enough – it's near universally missed from risk profiling exercises.

The final part of the puzzle in terms of pricing is the implementation costs. There is far more transparency around implementation costs, although this transparency is not deliberate – it's just easier to work out the cost model on implementation. Cost models on hardware and software licenses, and even cloud hosting, are more complex. Part of the cost model on the software in particular goes back to offsetting the vendor's upfront costs related to research and development. Implementation costs, on the other hand, are just "bodies", and you can already intuit a lot of these elements. You need to pay them (salary plus benefits), give them some equipment (which for these kind of staff essentially just means a £1,000/$1,200 laptop and a smartphone), give them a desk and some electricity, cover employer's tax obligations (employers National Insurance in the UK), and pay for their professional development.

The problems from the supplier's perspective is that they have to balance two factors – a) implementation time has a shelf life, and b) overworking the engineer is at best counterproductive, at worst ethically inappropriate. When you account for sick days, vacation, training, and other "blips" in availability, assuming that there are 16 sellable days in a month is about right. (These are based on UK days where there is more statutory vacation time, so in the US will see a greater "time inventory", but for now let's stick with 16 days.) In Chapter 1, I mentioned day rates for implementation engineers at an average of £1,200/$1,440 per day. If we stick with that, the total billing capacity per engineer is £19,200/$23,040 per month, which multiplies out to £230k/$294k per year.

This seems like a lot, but it really is not when you factor in the cost of labour. The supplier will see a healthy margin from this endeavour when things go smoothly – but remember that a good chunk of the smoothness from this project is dependent on the supplier's estimates for the fixed-price work being correct. This is where things can start to go wrong from the supplier, and when things go wrong for the supplier – even though the supplier should isolate you from it – as we've said previously, you as the customer can (and do) get affected.

In order for the supplier to make maximum margin, they have to sell exactly the number of budgeted capacity days (macro), and have the engineer work exactly the number of days allocated in the project plan (micro). Any fewer days sold (macro) and the supplier is paying the engineer to be at work for a day that's not being billed. Any more days worked (micro) and the supplier is reaching into their own pocket to offset the incorrect estimate (for example, it should have been a 72-day project, but 90 days have been spent). Because of the very large costs in real-terms, even small variations in terms of availability or estimates have a big impact in terms of cash.

Hopefully you can see how it's important that the supplier is given the opportunity to come up with correct estimates, but there is another factor in that the supplier is competing for the work and their perception of price will be a factor. It is easy enough to look at a quote as supplier and trim off "x%" because you have a hunch it'll be materially important in actually winning the bid. (I refer you back to Chapter 1 where spoke about how eye-wateringly expensive customer acqui-sition is – suppliers are *hugely* motivated to win your bid because they are obliged to pour enormous effort into getting to a point where they are able to present their proposal to you even though there's a better-than-evens chance they won't win the work.)

In summary, don't read too much into the apparently mas-sive day rates charged for implementation, because once you work the numbers, those rates are not as "enriched" as they seem. For margins on the rest of the solution, the supplier is not making much margin the hardware and commodity software that might be involved and is largely doing this as a convenience factor. There is healthy margin in vertically or horizontally specialised software. What the supplier is looking to sell you is that specialised software delivered through custom implementation. Finally, be aware that cloud solutions are outsourcing – consider the total cost, and do proper risk modelling around sudden failure (usually bankruptcy/insolvency) of the cloud partner.

Commoditisation vs Specialisation

We've spoken a lot in the previous sections about this idea of commoditisation, and for our purposes here what we mean by commoditisation is the interchangeability of parts such that price becomes the core differentiator. Practically, the only way to differentiate on price is to have a lower price. (This doesn't apply to Veblen goods, such as a Rolls Royce where the demand goes up as the price goes up – businesses don't ordinarily buy Veblen goods.) This is where we get the concept of the "race to the bottom from". That process of commoditisation cuts both ways, because in order to drive the price down, you have to mush and homogenise everything about the offer in order to make the arithmetic work. You don't get "special" when commoditising.

What you're paying for when you specialise – in the context of IT systems implementation – is advice. That higher margin goes directly into allowing the supplier to hire people who know what they are doing. If you're a supplier, you can also nudge your margin up a bit more by getting larger as typically people will feel that a large supplier is less likely to screw up a project than a smaller supplier would be – as such that higher cost can be justified through perception of a greater management of risk. (I remain unconvinced about this justification.)

Factors like growth in cloud outsourcing have a tendency to smush down the pricing across the whole market as the way cloud solutions are sold at least "flirts" with the principles of commoditisation because of the (incorrect) perception that these solutions are cheaper in real terms. Be careful then of things that look like the supplier chasing the price downwards because – frankly – they should know better to chase after commoditisation of their solution within the context of their competition within the market. You should prefer suppliers that know their value, and know that given that they exist in a late-stage capitalism economy, the should be seeking to keep that margin healthy as a result.

The other factor about advice is that it's common enough to find customers who do not know that they are paying for advice and then don't listen to the bigger picture of what their supplier's engineers are telling them. Project implementation is applied consultancy – it is paying a day rate for someone with skills and experience you do not have to assess the state of your business and invent/implement a perfect-fit bespoke solution for you. You are paying that margin anyway – you might as well get some benefit out of it and milk the engineers who are within your business building your solution for what they're worth.

Special Note about the Word "Estimate"

Although this book looks to ensure that both customer and supplier are happy when an IT system is sold, there is a certain implication around legal disputes – or more ideally, how to avoid them. One word that does cause problems is the use of the word "estimate".

Suppliers will put the word "estimate" on quotes on line items related to implementation effort. In fairness, these line items are always "estimates" – we've spoken at length in this chapter as to how a key part of pricing the project is educated guesswork. However, those of you who have been "lucky" enough to find themselves in court on matters of commercial disputes will know that a lot can be made of a single word, even if that word does not appear in the actual contract but instead appears anywhere within any of the documents related to the project.

Running alongside this is the issue that it's relatively rare for the contract to explicitly say "this is a fixed price project – you (the customer) will not pay more than the price written here". Often, the fact the project is fixed price is left open to interpretation. We talk more about contracts in Chapter 5, but you would do well to ensure materials related to costing do explicitly specify the fixed price nature of the solution, as opposed to implying the project is effectively delivered as time and materials.

Anyway, looking at the word "estimate", it is very important that you quantify this word in some way wherever you see it. A supplier may well be making an estimate, but you and the supplier need to agree (and write down) what you mean by estimate. Projects do change as they run – something we go into much more in Chapter 6 – but you do need to control this element. Don't forget as well that some suppliers are motivated to win the project and may be presenting quotes that are overly optimistic on the hope that flagging them as "estimates" provides them with a "get out of jail free" card.

It is risky to sign a contract where it says something like: "Implementation: 20 days (estimated)". You should agree with the supplier that estimates fall within a range, and I would suggest something like 5%–7.5% "wobble" on estimates is OK. But, to be clear, this needs to be clear within the documentation. The supplier can either present some text that says: "Implementation 18.5–21.5 days", or the supplier can say "20 days (estimated)" but somewhere else in that document is needs to say something like "XYZ Supplier agrees estimated values will not exceed 7.5% above estimate without written authorisation". (You can then follow this rabbit hole as much as you like, as in a framework agreement with you and the supplier you can express the process around that written authorisation, and reference that process in the document.)

However, it is *absolutely essential* that these rules are adhered to without exception. What can happen in a dispute is that you can produce ten documents that say "Estimated values will not exceed …" and then on the eleventh document omit that and now the supplier is arguing that estimates no longer have constraints. This can be tricky as it's easy to have legal guidance when signing those original framework agreements, and then have non-legal people quickly dashing off wording on documentation produced as the project runs without oversight on the actual documents that end up being presented as evidence in court.

Calculating the "TCO" Price

As mentioned before, suppliers are hugely motivated to sell their solution to you, and as such how pricing is presented as a sort of "industry standard" is not directly helpful to allowing you, the customer, to understand the total cost of ownership (aka "TCO") of the solution over the long term. This is not done with bad intentions – it's just pricing psychology. There is always pressure to bring your perception of the price down because the supplier is always bidding blind against their peers, and it's easier to present a proposal for £200k, and have the customer eventually come to the realisation it'll cost £100k a year to run it than it is to present a proposal that has "£1.2 million" written on it.

However, from your perspective, you need to know what you are in for and you do need that final price. It's therefore important to work with the supplier to get them to produce the price, which they will do, you just will need to ask them. (Of course, we're going to set-up a competition for vendors to bid for the work, which we'll cover in the next section, so practically you'll need to ask all of them.)

When do this, you do also need to broaden out the proposal to get the supplier(s) to present a view as to some other aspects that are often not included in a "total cost of ownership" application.

In the first instance, some suppliers can get a bit sketchy about including pricing for testing and training systems. When you build a system, you *always* need a separate, parallel system for testing and you *usually* need a separate training system. The test system is critical because it is (fatally) bad practice to modify systems whilst they are in active operational use. We talk about this more in Chapter 10, but for now the headline is that there are always three systems in play. The supplier builds the system on their own "development" environment. This "build" is then deployed onto a test system, which you as the customer have to sign off. Once you have signed it off, this build then gets deployed on the live system. (This live system is often called "production".) The issue is that these environments all have a cost. The cost for the development environment is borne by the supplier as a cost-of-doing-business. The live system is what you're buying, so you're obviously paying for that. The test system can sometimes end up being an afterthought, so you need to make sure that is clearly priced up in the proposals. Whilst training can be done on live environments, it's common enough for a training environment to be created – again, you need to check the cost of this is including in the proposal.

In the second instance, the proposal process tends to fixate on the initial delivery, whereas you are buying a complex piece of "equipment" that will likely spend at least a decade in the business being used every day. (The life of the sorts of systems we're discussing in this book should have a lifespan of around 10–15 years.) At time goes on, the system will need changing. Some of that change will come from the fact that the vendor will be releasing new versions. Sometimes these version changes can be quite radical – so radical in fact that the system you are in needs to be scrapped and you need to start over. (This is not a great position to find yourself in, and unhappily not one you get much visibility over in the early days.) Most of the changes through will be smaller maintenance changes and bug fixes. You though likely will want to make changes as new organisational imperatives emerge. The initial system deployment is just the first waypoint on a more complex roadmap, and it's important to get visibility of this right from the start. This segues into a more complex topic around IT strategy, and broader strategy questions are beyond the scope of this book, but your supplier (if they want to genuinely be that partner that they say in their marketing materials) will be able to help you with this.

All of this process I call "evergreening". It's absolutely critical that you consider the system as something that needs regular maintenance from the IT equivalent of a gardener, rather than just being that single point of time of getting it in through the door and "then what".

The final part of the life of the system to consider is retirement. The reason why I say this to "end the loop" and define the system as a holistic unit with a start, middle, and an end. Practically, it's very difficult to visualise the needs of the business 10–15 years after deployment. Sometimes, this can be done – for example the owners may want to exit within 10 years and you may well find it's perfectly easy to conceive of the system as needing to be merged into a larger organisation within the systems life. However, for completeness your roadmap has to include the point that is the "end of the road".

Summary

This chapter has really been about this long-standing "trick" that IT suppliers (and I suspect all sellers of complex products) do in that the basis on which their pricing is based is obfuscated. The economics of IT systems provision is at its core very simple – you have to pay people to build the solution, those people cost £x and the supplier wants to make a profit.

Fixed price projects are absolutely key when talking about the types of projects used in this book. (Practically, it's unfair to ask a very small supplier to do a fixed price project, but in this context this is a good thing because you should not be asking a very small supplier to do this work – a larger supplier will be able to stomach a fixed price project.) It's also a bad idea to be looking at an "experimental" project without in-house IT decision making skills. If you want to do this, you should engage a fractional CTO.

Finally, whatever you are doing is a collaborative endeavour – which obviously leads to a situation where both of you need to look out for a win-win. This means that as well as getting the system you want, you ideally need to be mindful of making it so that they can make a profit out of the deal (if they're operating in good faith, at least).

Chapter 4

Finding a Supplier

By this point in the book, you're likely tuned in to the idea that my philosophy on how to have more success buying complex IT systems is to understand the supplier's motivations and imperatives at least as well as you know your own. We're going to continue this theme now into the principles involved in finding the "right fit" supplier for you for your organisation and your project.

Understanding the Sales Cycle

In Chapter 1, we learned that the process of selling into you as an IT system customer is an extremely expensive activity. The key factor as to why this is so expensive is that, generally speaking, you – the customer – are not interested in buying IT systems most of the time. Your job is to run your organisation, and sometimes the proper functioning of that organisation might involving investment in IT, but even then there is a sense that when it comes to buy something you are *obliged* to do it, rather than it being something you want to do with a glad heart.

Once you take that precept you can apply another, namely that senior management in an organisation are usually time poor and

 DOI: 10.4324/9781003427766-4

don't want to be interrupted. As a result, over the past 30 years it has become extremely difficult to interrupt senior stuff to engage them in IT systems procurement. Picture the scene, someone phones you up, gets through the gatekeeper (somehow) and says to you, "Tell me, are you thinking about buying a new ERP system?" "Not really …" and the call ends. (There is, however, a nonzero chance that you are interested in buying a new ERP system, which is why this sort of marketing persists – someone will answer that question in the affirmative, and so the whole merry-go-round keeps turning.)

What marketeers (and new business reps) happened upon about 10 years ago is that if interruption marketing doesn't work, "expertise marketing" does. The principle of this is that you produce content that is of value to your target market, they will engage with it within a broader arc of the sales cycle. You then take this content and splatter it everywhere you can, and offer it for free. This is why every IT system you look to buy will invariably try and get you to download a white paper in exchange for an email address and permission to contact you, or they will invite you to events, or webinars. As a result of this B2B (business-to-business) marketing has got very content heavy.

A typical sales cycle goes through something like these steps:

1. Satisfied – the customer has a solution that works for them (which not be a software solution),
2. Unconsciously dissatisfied – the customer knows something isn't quite right, but is not consciously aware what,
3. Consciously dissatisfied – the customer knows something isn't quite right, and knows what.
4. Expression of needs – the customer is able to express internally to stakeholders and externally to the market what pain it has,
5. Evaluation of solutions – the customer is able to listen to the market for solutions and evaluate those solutions in terms of the pain it has,

6. Resolution of concerns – the customer is going through a process "dating" a set of suppliers to ascertain whether the delivered solution will suit,
7. Decision – the customer has decided which supplier to choose,
8. Implementation – the customer is actively deploying the solution.

In those set of stages, any new business rep from a supplier is able to have conversations with the customer only in three of those stages. This is the case either when using interruption marketing, or with expertise marketing. The only advantage of expertise marketing comes in the transaction between unconscious and conscious dissatisfaction on the principle that the content coming from the supplier helping the customer understand exactly what their problem is – this process builds trust and "greases the wheels" such that that supplier has an advantage when going into later stages in the cycle.

The purpose of me going through this process with you is to try and get you – as the customer – more into the driving seat. When you are "expressing your needs", they are *your* needs as an organisation, and it is the supplier's job to listen to those. It's too easy for the supplier to blind you with science and push their solutions. Suppliers, at every phase of this cycle, are there to provide advice – again as per the last chapter the value that a supplier creates for you is "advice"; this is where the value is and how you and the supplier push away from commoditisation and race-to-the-bottom pricing and move towards a place of genuine partnership that delivers value.

What's happened though, holistically, is that interruption marketing has got so ineffective that the industry now biases everything towards expertise marketing. This creates its own race to the bottom – everyone's content looks the same, and genuine experts in most specialisms are as rare as hen's teeth. (This problem will undoubtedly get worse with generative AI like

Chat-GPT. For example, just an experiment I asked it to: "write me a blog post on why I should buy SAP Business One for UK-based midmarket manufacturing business" and out pops a perfectly serviceable article, although it's basically dross.) This makes finding the right supplier considerably harder as, as per the last chapter, it squashes down genuine expertise into a commodity play along with its "race to the bottom" pricing. As of the time of writing, it is almost impossible to find meaningfully useful content online – everyone is an expert, and everyone is saying the same thing.

A Quick Word on "BANT"

The above is the general shape to the purchasing process. The last factor to consider is the principle of "BANT". In order for a sales process to be successful, from the perspective of the supplier, the following needs to be in place:

1. Budget – the organisation has to be prepared to spend the money required to deliver the solution. As per the last chapter, it's important to ensure budget for the 10–15 years required to keep the system "alive", as opposed to just considering the initial implementation,
2. Authority – the person the salesperson is talking to has to have authority to sign the agreement.
3. Need – the stakeholders within the organisation have to agree that the organisation has a need (moreover, the stakeholders all have to agree what this needs is),
4. Timescale – the implementation of the solution has to be "timebound". Realistically, this means the supplier needs to know when they can invoice.

This is all very "supplier-focused", but the reason why I bring this up is because as a customer, this is the dance that you are engaged with, and if that dance does not suit where you and the organisation are at the time, you should not engage as all you will be doing is wasting your time as the relationship will not click into place. You will end up creating a whole load of paperwork and artefacts for something that amounts to a little more than an intellectual exercise, and you would likely have been able to make better use of that time. If you are not ready to invest £1 m/ $1.2 m over 15 years in an IT system, then don't start the process to buy one. If that's the case, you likely are more in a place to spend £10k/$12k on a formal scoping exercise (as per Chapter 2).

Making a Long-List of Suppliers

In order to go to market, you need to know what you're trying to buy. This is why Chapter 2 appears before this chapter, I should reiterate that it is *absolutely critical* that you write the specification before you go out to market.

Another thing to reiterate from Chapter 2 is that it's very important that you write the specification in a way that is agnostic as to the vendor. Two very common types of systems to buy are customer relationship management systems (CRM), and enterprise resource management systems (ERP). When you write the specifications, you should write it from the perspective of what you need them to do, as opposed to how the vendor makes their system do what it does. This will make it harder to find a supplier as the market is configured in a very vendor-centric manner, however it will get you the better results.

For example, as of the time of writing, for midmarket businesses the two optimal CRM vendors are considered to be Salesforce and Microsoft. It's not important to write the specification along the line of "Salesforce lets you create a customer like …" or "Dynamics let's you report on sales like …". The specification should be written like "The system we design MUST let you create a customer …", or "When running a report, the output MUST show …". (Just for the sake of completeness, the two optimal ERP system vendors are SAP and [again] Microsoft.)

If you know that you want to buy, for example "Salesforce Sales Cloud", accessing the market is reasonably easy because vendors will create a supplier ecosystem (aka "the channel") and will put considerable time, effort, and money into supporting suppliers to sell their solutions. However, this tends to "stratify" the constellation of suppliers that you can work with to be aligned to specific solutions. As a result, it's difficult to go and find suppliers and ask them to recommend a vendor because the people you're talking to are likely to specialise in whatever COTS product they've decided to specialise in and can't or won't offer advice as to which COTS solution is best, because as far as they're concerned they've already chosen which one is best.

The best solution to this in terms of cost and ease is to ask people who you trust for recommendations or referrals. It's important however that you don't just get one recommendation – you need to solicit informal advice from a reasonably broad base. This will start to get you a flavour of what the market looks like. This will also start to tune you into possible suppliers for implementation.

Looping back to the first part of this chapter, what these days does not work so well is Googling things like "best CRM for midmarket businesses" as the organic listings tend to be stuffed with content optimised for content marketing. Remember, the only effective way for B2B businesses to reach you as a customer is by publishing "expert" content – the result being that of the time of writing in 2024, nearly all content online is the same low-level, homogenised, basic content that is of little use. For example, I just now Googled "best CRM for midmarket businesses UK", and all of the results in pages 1, 2, and 3 are simply giving the wrong or bad advice.

One of the worst places to look, ironically, is the Gartner G2 website. It's ironic because this takes something that is the best place to look – the Gartner Magic Quadrants – and strips way the actual advice part. If you're unfamiliar, a Magic Quadrant is a way of visualising the competency of a solution against its peers. It's a chart designed with four regions that considers completeness of vision from "less complete" to "more complete" on the x-axis, and ability to execute from "less able" to "more able" on the right. The four quadrants are: "leaders", "challengers", "visionaries", and "niche players", with leaders being the most able to execute against a most complete vision, compared to their peers. You can usually get a good enough answer to what vendor to select by choosing anything from the "leaders" section, although you should expect premium pricing in this section.

You will usually be able to find a Magic Quadrant for every classification of product that you want, however they are themselves research reports that Gartner charges for. Where there is a bit of a hack is that when a vendor gets on a Magic Quadrant they tend to publicise it, with permission to reproduce the chart. With a bit of Googling about, you can find the chart and from there you can find out the other vendors in the space that you are looking for. (The Google Image Search tends to do well with this, although I've also had some luck with ChatGPT.) However, do check the dates of the reports associated with the charts, and also watch out for situations where Gartner can produce highly niched versions of the Magic Quadrants that might not match what you are looking for. You may also get some success using Chat-GPT for this – although as of the time of writing this tool is very new and your mileage may vary.

The reason why the Gartner G2 website is not as good as it could be is that it includes all the vendors from the Magic Quadrants, and then a whole load of vendors that are not in them, but then doesn't add any insights or intelligence to the listing. What you're left with is a huge list of products in the space, but it leaves you no further on as to which one you should buy. (The reason why I'm haranguing Gartner G2 specifically is because people read that it's by "Gartner" and then buy into it on that basis – it's not as good or as useful as the name implies.)

At this point, you should have some steer from referrals and recommendations which is then informed by products sitting in the "Leaders" section in an appropriate Magic Quadrant. You are looking to find two products that you should be able to successfully match up to your specification and then engage suppliers around. You can think of both of these options as a "Coca-Cola" choice and a "Pepsi" choice – you're aiming for two market leaders that both make competent products, both of which will likely meet your needs in similar (but different) ways.

No Magic Quadrant? What about Non-leaders?

If there isn't a Magic Quadrant in the space you need, it's going to be down to you to find the leaders in the space. This is likely to happen if the type of product you need is highly specialised, and there's no margin in Gartner in producing a Magic Quadrant for it. (IT systems supply really is all about margin, isn't it?)

By all means, however you're sourcing the long-list of vendors, you don't have to choose the leaders in the space. There may be some very good niche players in the space, for example. The issue is that evaluating leaders requires less technical skill than evaluating non-leaders, and in organisations without in-house IT leadership that evaluation can be difficult. For a major investment in a system that will be in daily use within your business for 10–15 years, it is absolutely critical that the right vendor is chosen. As the, now very old, saying goes "No one ever got fired for buying IBM". Today you can replace the "IBM" with whatever market leader you want, but the only reason why you can do that is that the leaders in the market tend to have a lower chance of screwing up. That's not to say the supplier won't screw up though (i.e. the implementers), but then that's why you're reading this book.

Next ... The Suppliers

At this point, you should have two vendors in mind, and you are aiming to find three suppliers for each. It's likely that by socialising your request for referrals and recommendations that you have two or three of these in place. To fill out the list, the best thing to do next is go back to the vendor and look at their "partner directories". As per the above discussion on the quality of online content related to complex IT systems sales, it's now quite difficult to find suppliers by looking for search results on Google.

Vendors will typically look to enrich the quality of their partner ecosystems, as it creates an more broadly larger and effective sales force – part of that activity is referring customers like you into their partners, on the hope that those partners will become your suppliers. To that end, vendors will typically publish a directory on their website of partners who they are happy to direct you to.

Typically vendors do not do a great deal of due diligence on the quality of their partners. Vendors will set some sort of bar that suppliers have to get over, but they are commercially-motivated bars, not governance-motivated bars. That's not a criticism, but it's something to be aware of – the supplier's relationship with the vendor, unless they are a very large supplier, will be quite "hands-off". Vendors like to pile up huge quantities of partners as it increases their reach.

When you have suppliers in mind, the most important first action is to confirm the jurisdiction of their legal entity, and confirm their scale. Confirming the legally incorporated entity is easily enough done with desk research. (If you're struggling to discern the legal entity behind a supplier, companies will usually surface their incorporated entity's details through the privacy policy on their website.)

Some suppliers will operate from overseas locations and this is risky if you need to take them to court. For example, if you operate in the UK and choose a UK supplier, you can take them to a court in the UK easily enough. (At least, the threat/possibility is readily apparent.) If you operate in the UK and choose a supplier based in, for example, Finland, legal action will get an order of magnitude more complicated. No one wants to end up suing anyone – but it's better to be in a position where you can if you need to, as opposed to being effectively unable to because of the complexities of cross-jurisdiction litigation.

What you are looking to do is get a guestimate as to the number of employees in the supplier's business. You can do this with LinkedIn, and any supplier you're looking at will automatically qualify themselves in or out using their LinkedIn presence. A business big enough to warrant your business will have their LinkedIn presence sorted out. If you can't find the supplier on LinkedIn, it's likely too small to warrant the business.

The employee size metric is a balancing act. Suppliers with a large number of employees are less likely to give you the sort of "white glove" or "you're the most special customer in the world" treatment. Suppliers will a small number of employees may well crawl over broken glass to make you happy (especially if you are a good customer), but if something does go wrong they can often be under-resourced. You want something that is a little larger than "boutique", but no so large that the owners are disconnected from the day-to-day operations of the business. I would say that 50–100 employees is about right for the types of systems discussed in this book, but you can go down to 35 and up to 150 and still be in the right area.

In summary, it is always better to create a long-list of suppliers using recommendations and referrals from people who are in your network. It will likely be difficult to get the six you need (three each for the two solutions that you are considering) – this is when you would go to the vendors to source the remaining companies through their partner networks.

Initial Discussions

Now that you have identified the long-list of suppliers, you're now ready to have the initial conversations with them. The best way to approach this is to operate as if you are interviewing for a senior hire within the business. Each of the suppliers will want to engage with you as if you are a sales prospect that they are looking to sell into, and as such you will be invited to enter a process that they understand intimately and have done many times before – they are much more practiced at selling into companies like yours than you are at buying from companies like theirs, and as such you need to gently subvert the process more into your terms. One way to do this is to reframe the "buying" process as if it were an interview for a senior hire, something your organisation is likely to have more experience with. (There is a lot of similarly here too – a senior hire will cost you a lot of money over the long term, will/ should bring enormous benefits, and certainly will cause horrendous problems if you make the wrong choice.) Running the process like this will also allow you to smooth out the differences in how the suppliers engage, which will allow you to see each candidate suppliers plusses and minuses more easily.

If you're following my recommendations in this book, having been through Chapter 2 you should now either be in the mood to create or have created a decent functional specification. Having this document – or rather, having a *good* functional specification – will position you as being quite unusual compared to other clients that the supplier has dealt with, because most organisations commissioning complex IT systems are not able to write good functional specifications. I will just mention – before sending the functional specification, the supplier should sign a non-disclosure agreement.

The way that the sales process works typically works is that the presales engagement will start off with quite a light technical input and progress through to a deeper input as both parties work out whether the engagement has legs. If you can forgive me for being stereotypical, this means that you will be meeting people who are more "salesy" at the start and then more "techie" as you go on. It may be in the very first meetings there are no technical people involved as the salesperson will want to quality in the basics of BANT (budget, authority, need, and timescale) to see whether you are a real opportunity or not. Once the supplier does feel you ultimately are able to commission the project, a technical person should be in subsequent meetings – we're about to come on to this point, but that person should be someone who will have day-to-day involvement in the project.

This approach is fine, but as I said we're subverting the typical process in this recommended process that I'm taking you through here. What you want to do at the initial stages is get each supplier that you talk to validate the business imperatives of what you are trying to do. As you're going to be talking more to salespeople first, those individuals will have the sort of business analysis skills that are required to understand how to fit the solution that they sell and understand to the organisation that you happen to be. As mentioned, you have this specification but at this stage you don't necessarily need the salesperson to be that engrossed in the detail within. What you are getting those is, ideally, six specialist business analysts coming into the building and talking with you and your team about what you are trying to achieve as an organisation. It's critical at this point that you're able to process this input effectively. An excellent outcome at this point is if something emerges from this process that undermines the whole endeavour and obliges you to "go back to the drawing board", because you haven't spent any real money at this point (in comparison to the projected cost at least).

Coming back to this idea that this process is effectively an interview process by any other name, when the actual implementation is happening the supplier will deploy quite a small team. Even for quite a big spend – for example, £250k/$300 – it's likely you will only see a small team of perhaps two or three people do the actual work. It's critical that at this initial stage you are getting to meet the people who the supplier will allocate to the project as you will need to work closely with them to deliver the solution. Although these individuals are external to the business and the engagement is an outsourced one, what you are really doing is renting expertise to create a team that is owned by both you the customer and the supplier. Those engineers are those who will have to read the functional specification in proper detail, not least of all because you want the opportunity for someone to "check your homework" with regards to what's actually in the specification.

The supplier will, in fairness, not be able to guarantee that the engineers you interview are ultimately those allocated to the project, but they should be able to offer something on a best endeavours basis. You may meet some resistance from this, but in all honestly the supplier should realise this process is a benefit from them as the more you get to know the engineers and the more you like them and build up trust, the more likely you will be to select them as the people who are going to do the work.

As we did at the initial business-focused part of this process, working with the engineering teams is where you will be able to get some "free" consultancy around the technical implementation. As this is more of a technical mode of operation, it will be beneficial to get the stakeholders within your organisation more closely involved. For example, the CFO might not fully understand the day-to-day operations of the warehouse, but the warehouse manager will, and they will be able to quickly or qualify out any recommendations or concerns from the supplier's engineers at this early stage.

This early stage work is absolutely critical, and this is why we are loading this project approach up with this large amount of workup-front. The analogy, for example, is an architect who draws a house and reverses the elevation left-to-right. It is far cheaper for the site manager to notice this on Day 1 before anyone has finished breakfast and started building the thing than it is for the customer to notice the house is backwards on the day of handover.

To tie this together, the very first meeting is likely just to be with a salesperson. The meeting after that should have the project manager who will run the project. The third and later technical meetings should have at least the lead engineer who will be involved day-to-day on the project. I won't go through in detail here what you are looking for in the interview, as it's not that deep. You simply need to get a feel as to whether the supplier understands your business, understands the technical requirements, and whether you actually like and can work with the personnel who happen to be in front of you at that point – that is, it is just a matter of sensing whether confidence is building or not, just as you would do when you were doing a normal interview.

This may seem like a lot of work to do this not just with one but ideally six suppliers, but again over a 10–15 year period this system could cost you a huge sum of money and will be absolutely critical to the operation of the business. The more time you can invest now is guaranteed to pay dividends over the long term.

Project Management Methodologies

We do need to quickly touch on a due diligence piece around project management. We are going to talk about project management methodologies in much more detail in Chapter 6, but just in case you're eagerly interviewing suppliers without reading the whole book first this point is important.

You should discard any supplier that does not talk-the-talk about project management. A supplier will typically have a preferred methodology. The actual methodology they want to use is not hugely important, although it can be a factor. If you have a management team that is very used to PRINCE2 and you have two equally matched suppliers to consider, one that loves PRINCE2 and one that loves PMP, the PRINCE2 supplier might have the edge.

A Quick Word about Tenders/Requests for Proposals

If I may quickly cover off this point about tenders/requests for proposals (RFPs). The process I've outlined above will no doubt come across as quite involved, and perhaps makes you think about formal tendering or RFP processes. These types of processes do not work effectively for midmarket businesses as they do not have the internal resourcing required to receive bids in this way. This is, after all, the point of the first part of this book – to teach you how to go to market safely even though your organisation is missing the resources needed to run a formal bid process.

Proposals and Back to Scoping

In a normal staff hiring interview process, you already more or less know the "price" that you are willing to pay for the work, save for some negotiation on the final package. In the quasi-interview process that we've been talking about so far, you don't know the price, and this is now the most important next phase.

We spoke about scoping exercises in Chapter 2, and it is now likely that you are at the stage where you need to commission one. You also need to decide which solution to buy in terms if the vendor. For example, if you asked three suppliers to talk you about SAP Business One and three suppliers to talk to you about Microsoft Dynamics, you need to decide which of them to choose.

Of the six (or so) suppliers that you interview, you should invite proposals in from those you like with the purpose of obtaining an indicative price. The suppliers will all be keen to do a scoping exercise because they are highly beneficial to them in terms of moving you through the sale process, but you should push each of them to present an indicative price prior to commissioning any for them to undertake a scoping exercise. In terms of the content of those proposals, 90% of it is likely to be more of a sales-y style that will be of less use to you, especially as you would have been through and got to know each of them quite well. Again, as we went through in Chapter 3, you should push the suppliers to provide total cost of ownership prices over a 10–15 year timescale, but do get this broken down in a phased way so that you can be certain how much you're likely to spend in terms of initial licences, initial implementation, then operational costs and maintenance costs over the long term.

In doing this process, you will get a spread of likely costs, and those costs are almost certainly going to cluster. If the costs do not cluster, the supplier is likely to have made a mistake in the estimate, or there is some machination at play either low-balling or high-balling the price. Either way, it's up to you how to you want to smooth out outliers.

The question as to which vendor (as opposed to supplier) you need to choose is going to be very much down to you at this point, and meaningful differences in the price/pricing structure may be something that you find relevant. It is likely that you will know which one you prefer, having spent what will by this point will be a highly decent amount of time "kicking the tyres/tires" of each of them, with experts in the room. You will know the one that you like best.

Once you have a vendor and a supplier that you like, you need a scope of work and a timeline. Of all the different families of dispute an IT customer and IT supplier can get into, disputes around scope are by far the most common (By 'scope' here, I mean the actual project deliverables, i.e. "the scope of work") – this is a separate concept from a "scoping exercise", the output of which is supposed to ascertain the scope.). As alluded to in Chapter 3, any document that is exchanged between customer and supplier can surface in legal proceedings, and the proposal you receive even before the work has been scoped properly can be one of these complicating documents. We talk more about this in the next chapter, but in essence you need to formally supercede the proposal with a scope of work. As per Chapter 2, the best way to do this is through a shortform consultancy engagement called a "scoping exercise", and again in Chapter 2 I mentioned that this scope might cost around 5%–10% of the final price. (By final price here I mean *only* the initial implementation costs – not the multiplied out 10–15 year "total cost of ownership" price.) As such, this is likely the thing to do next – once you have a vendor and you have a preferred supplier, it's time to engage them.

You don't absolutely have to pay them to do a scoping exercise, but the outcome that you want is you want them to effectively redraft your functional specification as their own and attach a formal scope of works, a formal timeline, and a formal final price. For them to do this properly, it's fair of them to expect to be paid to do this work. We mentioned the inherent risk in the words "estimate" in Chapter 3, but I'll mention it again here – if the suppliers puts the word "estimate" in that document anywhere, it is critical to formally define what you both understand about that word. You should not allow doubt that a supplier-drafted specification, supplier-drafted scope of work, and supplier-drafted price is anything other than a fixed-price commitment. That same risk around estimated pricing can crop up with estimated timelines too. If the supplier is able to tell you how much something will cost to build, they are able to tell you when elements of the delivery will land. Those three documents – the agreed final specification, the agreed price, and the agreed timeline, are now all ready for signoff.

Summary

This chapter continues the work that we looked at in the last chapter – that is, looking closer at the internals of how IT systems supplier operate so that we might better understand how to buy from them (and how we might work with them as we go forward). In particular, we spoke about the marketing and purchasing cycle.

When choosing a supplier, it's important that we take a whole market view and build a decent long-list of suppliers to choose from. Recommendations from people that we know in our personal network are hugely important. (Apart from anything else, searching online now – whilst hugely important in B2B sales – this approach produces difficult results that are very "spammy" and low quality.)

A scoping exercise is the only practical way to de-risk complex projects. (They also give you and the organisation a lot of insights as to what it is you are trying to build and why.) From there, it's a matter of formalising the work to be done and going forward into the project in a good shape.

Chapter 5

Commissioning

Now that you know what you're building and have agreed a price, you're now ready to enter into an agreement to do the actual work. This chapter represents the end of the first part of the book where you're deciding what to buy and who to buy it from – in the next chapter we start the second part of the book where we look at how to manage the successful delivery of the project.

The Contract

At the end of the introduction to the book, I added a quick note that nothing in this book constitutes legal advice. I'll reiterate this if I may – I am not a lawyer, and any advice that I provide in this book is designed to be guidance to increase your chances of a successful complex IT systems delivery.

The supplier will provide you with a contract to sign, and it is essential that you get your lawyer to formally advise you on this contract. That said, there are some things that I have seen lawyers miss – they're experts in contract law, not dyed-in-the-wool IT systems implementors, and that's the purpose of the rest of this chapter. You might want to get them to read through this chapter, and I'll try and keep it short to keep the billing down!

DOI: 10.4324/9781003427766-5

What Are Disputes For?

Any two parties are free to agree amongst themselves any action or non-action as they so wish, providing it is legal. This means that if a customer and supplier are in dispute, there is no reason why those two parties can't decide any resolution they like. If the parties can't agree, one recourse they have is to ask a third party to arbitrate a decision for them. Taking someone to court is a form of binding arbitration – you ask the court to look at the evidence on both sides and then make a decision for them, that the parties then have to carry out because that decision is binding.

If the matter is purely civil (i.e. nothing actually criminal has occurred), the court tends to care only about "tortious loss", which for the purposes of this book given the subject is IT systems procurement, this effectively boils down to "loss of money". You may feel that your dispute is about time, or reputation, or some other way in which your organisation has lost out, but realistically you would struggle to get the court to grapple with anything other than the core issue of "did you get what paid for?". The other major issue with going to court is that no one knows what words will come out a judge's mouth before they say them. This means you can have the world's strongest case, a "guaranteed win", only to find yourself getting surprisingly minced at the final judgement.

Effectively, legal disputes only work in situations where you want to get the money that you have spent back. The problem with this is that you do not actually get a working system at the end of it. You can spend six months commissioning a system, a year implementing a system, and spend £250k/$300 on the project, and a the end of it, the system does not work. If you take them to court and win – that process will take at least a year – you may get your money back, but you have still wasted two-and-a-half years. You will also spend a heart-stopping amount of money on legal fees, which you may not get back.

Going to court is always a disastrous process for solving IT systems disputes for the reason that any victory is somewhat Pyrrhic in that you don't get the system you wanted in the first place.

Nowadays, the legal profession is keen to see alternative dispute resolutions measures, and there are now more options for helping parties resolve disputes without putting the matter in front of a judge. The most common of those is mediation, which acts to cool the heat between the parties. A solution I particularly like, although it's quite uncommon, is technical project remediation which is where a technical specialist is jointly appointed to shepherd the project through to completion. Both of these mediation-based approaches increase the chances of you getting a working system (if such a thing is possible and the project isn't an absolute disaster), but there is much less chance you will get your money back through mediation as ultimately the supplier is still looking to transfer the actual value of the system from themselves to yourselves, whereby you pay for that privilege.

Jurisdiction

We looked at this in the last chapter, but to reiterate – it's essential to ensure that the supplier is within the same legal jurisdiction as yourselves – ultimately you need the option of taking them to court to be as smooth as possible if you need to do that. Court action across boundaries of jurisdiction adds significant complexity, and any cost benefit you may find in working with a supplier in another country will get nullified by this factor if you need to take them to court.

Resources

Just to keep piling on the problems with taking companies to court, whether you win or not doesn't have a definitive bearing on whether you get paid. This is a factor in why in the last chapter I was keen to press that the supplier you choose should be at a certain scale – they have to be able to pay you if you win, ideally without obliging the principals in the business to go off and sell their assets to cover the cost. Take some time to assess whether you feel the supplier has enough cash in the bank to refund you should it come to it.

Insurance

I've had debates with clients about this before, but as far as I am concerned, it is essential to get proof that the supplier has sufficient insurance to cover reimbursing the project costs, if it comes to it. Insurance takes the heat of a situation – it allows the supplier to hand-off dealing with the "problem" that is you as a client to a third-party who is less "emotional" and is seeing if they can reasonably avoid paying out money as rather than struggling as hard as they possibly can not to pay out money. You (or ideally, your lawyer) should check the insurance paperwork to make sure it is satisfactory, and the contract should seek to agree that proper insurance will be held for the life of the project.

Discovery

I will mention this point because it tends to come with more complete IT strategy work and it's often a blind-spot for smaller organisations. It's important that you have a separate system that archives any email that comes into or out of your organisation, separate to the user's mailboxes. This sort of archive can be invaluable when resolving any kind of dispute (e.g. HR disputes), but in this context it's particular relevant because if there is a dispute, any email related to the project is expected to be given to the other side in litigation through a process known as discovery.

This creates a lot of complexity in litigation because (a) you have to find them, (b) you have to interpret them, and (c) any one of them can subvert your story/case that you're putting forward. Finding them is half the battle – which is why it is helpful to have an archive where you can just search for the internet domain name of the supplier and turn up any email that was sent. Interpreting them is often very difficult, as you have to wade through emails like "How was golf this weekend?" to find ones like, "I agree we don't need this feature, but we're happy to pay for it regardless".

In summary then – you should have an email archive, but in any case if you're going into litigation you will need to find and turn over all of those emails. Setting up a filing system where all the emails can be put into one place where they can be referred back to is a worthy best practice at this point.

Intellectual Property

Matters around intellectual property (IP) tend to be more of an issue with fully bespoke software, which we'll look at properly in Chapter 8, but just for completeness I will mention this here.

Historically, there used to a problem in the world of IT systems supply where the customer would commission a project, and the supplier would retain the IP. (Effectively, the customer would be granted a perpetual license by the supplier to use a system that they commissioned and paid for.) This is less of an issue now, as when the industry was younger there was a perception that this sort of highly specialised IP was more valuable than it ultimately is, but it is still an issue today.

It's very important that the intellectual property of the bespoke work that you commission transfers to you at specific control points. You obviously can't own the IP in the vendor's work, but any work that is done by the supplier as specific/ custom implementation work you can own the IP of. By default, the IP will lodge with the entity doing the work as it is done, so the supplier will own the IP until it is transferred. A fair way to do this is that when the invoices covering a piece of work are paid, the IP transfers.

This work will require specific support from a lawyer with intellectual property experience. It's generally not enough in a contract to specify an *intent* to transfer IP at control points. You will almost certainly need some sort of "ceremony" to actually do the IP transfer in a way that it's defensible. This is especially true if the organisation looks to be sold in a management buy-out or trade sale, or even ultimately looks to list publicly.

Escrow and Failure

Along the lines of the IP issue is that of the actual work that is being done. We'll talk about this much more in Chapter 11, but again for completeness here there is a risk of failure during implementation, which you have to manage out. In broad terms – and again we'll go this properly in a later chapter – you need an escrow agreement whereby the work the supplier is doing is being put into escrow as they do it. If the supplier becomes insolvent or goes bankrupt, you can go to the escrow provider, arrange to be passed copies of the work that they have done out of escrow, and then source another provider to continue the work. This step may be overly complex or impractical for your project, but please do have the discussion about potential mitigation of this risk before signing the contract.

What to Sign Off

To bring forward the discussion from the end of the last chapter, the five "artefacts" that describe the project are:

- The contract,
- The price,

- The functional specification,
- The scope of work,
- The project timeline.

The formal sign-off needs to be clear that the agreement is those five things, not anything that came before. Plus, those five items should be relatively immutable in that they can only be changed through a formal process. Again, with one eye to controlling risk from conflict, it is better to have a definite base rather than have exposure to things that might have been mentioned in passing and noted. These five items together notionally make up the "agreement".

Those five pieces all work together like gears in the machine. You, as the customer, need to be profoundly confident that the functional specification describes what you want. Hopefully there has been enough work done to qualify and requalify those outputs such that if a magic wand were waved and the system you wanted is just instantly before you, the functional specification would describe it exactly without surprises. (You can, and will, vary the project – we'll go through that in Chapter 9.)

The timeline and scope of work together, and you can think of them like perpendicular axes – timeline on the "x", and scope of work on the "y". Both elements relate to each other. Each item in the scope of work has to be addressed methodically and in turn, and you should expect to know when each item will be delivered by reference to the timeline. You can expect some resistance to "holding the supplier's feet to the fire" with regard to the timeline as suppliers do like to have some wiggle room. (Changes to scope should have a financial impact if they are major changes.)

In terms of how I've seen this process not be as tight as it should be, the thing that is usually correct is the contract as people tend to know they need to get a contract checked by a lawyer, and there usually is a good shared understanding of base practice within that discipline. Everything else can get overly loose.

We spoke in Chapter 3 about how dangerous the word "estimate" can be. I'll reiterate that again if I may – always ensure the word "estimate" is couched in language that makes it clearly quantifiable. Ensuring that, and being clear within the agreement that is a fixed price project is important. I have seen projects where there seemed to be a clear understanding that the project was fixed price, only have the supplier litigate on the basis that it was time and materials.

The next thing that tends to exist but be improperly defined is the functional specification. This document really does need to be precise, and I think that's fair to say as this document does describe that you are buying and if it is an imprecise document, how can you really know you will get the value you want from the system you are commissioning? Hopefully the work we've been through in this part of the book has got you to a point where you can create a really good, well-defined spec.

The last two pieces, the scope of work and the timeline, are the pieces that are often straight-up missing from the agreement at the point of sign-off. The next chapter sees the start of the second part of this book where we look at delivery as a whole, and we start that by talking about project management. The scope of work is simply a list, however you do that and it can just be an Excel file, of what features are going to be built. The supplier will have created a scope of work in order to determine the price – the process they go through is simply to note down each thing that needs doing and then just estimate the number of days each one will take, multiplied the estimate by the day rate, and that is the price. You need both create a sign-off-able version of that and then attach a deliverable timeline to it.

With all five pieces of that in place, you're ready to sign on the dotted line and get on with delivering your new IT system.

Summary

We've now got to the end of the part of the book where we're buying something, and moving into the part of the book that's about building something. When you do go out to get legal advice with regard to the contract, bear in mind that most lawyers are not experts in IT systems delivery. You ideally need to get advice that covers both angles of the endeavour.

We also touch in this chapter about dispute resolution. As an engineer, I always worry about risk, and I also enjoy fixing projects where the supplier relationship has broken down, so I tend to think about these topics at lot. (It's a big reason why I wrote this book.) In order to get a remedy from a failed supplier, you need know what they can actually pay you a remedy. This means they need to have enough money in the bank, and need to carry the right insurance.

The final issue around the arrangements with the supplier are matters related to intellectual property. Ultimately, if you're paying someone to do work, you should own the output.

Chapter 6

Project Management

"If you fail to plan, you are planning to fail."
– commonly attributed to Benjamin Franklin

We're now moving into Part 2 of the book where we look at the actual delivery of the system. We've done a lot of work in Part 1 to get to a point where the project has the most chance of success, and if we're not going to see success, the organisation has a defensible position with regards to remediation.

In this chapter we're going to look at project management. I cannot overstate the importance of effective project management in reaching a point of successful delivery. However, this isn't a project management book so we're going to take a broad look at the various different factors of managing projects and how you need to work with each of those factors.

In particular, it's critical that you as the customer do not actually do the project management piece. The supplier will do the project management, but taking a hands-off approach with regards to their project management would be a mistake – i.e. you need to be involved. What you need to do is navigate your way into a position where you have close supervision of their project management activities. We'll see how do to that as we go on.

DOI: 10.4324/9781003427766-6

How to Supervise the Project

Project management can be considered as having four aspects – defining the scope, planning the project, managing the project, and closing out the project. We've therefore done a huge chunk of project management work in the previous five chapters as all of Part 1 was about creating a proper scope of works. The next element – managing the project – is a bit like steering a rocket to hit a target. You have to take continual measurements of position, speed, and trajectory and make small adjustments to increase the likelihood that the rocket will actually hit the target.

As we mentioned in Chapter 4, a supplier will have a pre-ferred methodology, and it doesn't matter too much what that is, although it's helpful if your project team is comfortable with it. To reiterate, you're not the one doing the project manage-ment – the supplier is, but you have to maintain a supervisory position over that process.

In order to do that, both parties must agree at the beginning of the project on the shape of the project board, the frequency and type of "touchpoints" used, and the artefacts that will be created as the project proceeds.

The project board needs to comprise people from your or-ganisation and the supplier's organisation, and you should look to be quite creative with regards to composition of the board. One of the issues with delivering systems like this is that people are busy and they have their own jobs to do. This is not helped by the fact that, unless you live it every day, building IT systems is a pretty boring activity. You can think of this as people having Type A activities (i.e. what they are directly paid to do, e.g. managing a warehouse, keeping the books), and Type B activities (i.e. this IT systems project). Type A activities are "core mission" – doing these directly involve delivering on the or-ganisation's core mission. Type B activities are "hygiene fac-tors" – these are things the organisation must do to keep itself safe and healthy. You can think of there being an elastic band tethered to people such that when they are over in a Type B space, they are always feeling pressure pulling them back to Type A activities. Culture can have an impact on this as well.

Some people quite like the variety and can handle it well. They may like the distraction and challenge of spending some time doing Type B activities when they spend most of their week on Type A. However, some people operate on a spectrum of "stress" through to "resentment" when asked to spend time on Type B activities.

You need to build a project board that is biased towards the former, and takes input but doesn't require too much involvement from the latter. This may not elegantly line up with the business imperatives behind the project – for example, the warehouse manager may be an absolutely key stakeholder in the project, but if getting them to spend a day a week on the project is like pulling teeth, you will have to find a way around that. (This is a fact of life of software projects – all software projects are like this, universal buy-in is a myth.)

The head of the project board is a crucial role and this must be an individual who is more than able to run the project, and who has the respect and buy-in of all the stakeholders regardless of how the stakeholder feels about having to spend time on the project. (There is a difference between the stakeholder not wanting to spend time on the project, and just being outwardly hostile towards the project. You shouldn't have stakeholders that don't believe in what the organisation and project board are trying to do – but hopefully you would have worked that out in the preliminary specification phases.) That head of the project board may well be the organisations COO – the person in this role is likely a good fit given the size of organisations that this book is looking to support combined with the size of the projects that we're discussing.

To reiterate, the project board should have representatives from the supplier on it. This will usually be the designated "project/customer success" person at the supplier, and the lead engineer. I quite like the term "customer success", but it's relatively modern and the supplier will probably describe themselves as the project manager or project lead. Language is important in business, and it can be helpful to "program" the supplier to think of that person as having a role related to success as it gains buy-in, and allows the head of the project board to frame the work the supplier does as being related to the joint success of the project.

The supplier's project manager will be doing the day-to-day project management, which is essentially a process of ensuring that the work is being done on the days that it is supposed to be done, and flagging up emerging risks to the project board for evaluation. A risk should be a simple issue like "we need to change this" or "we need to change that" – that is, small variations. (We talk more about variations in Chapter 9.) The value of the engineering lead being on the board when it meets (which we'll look at next) is that the board can ask technical queries and get rapid answers back.

The board exists to measure and evaluate the project trajectory, and sign off any changes that needs to be made. This is done by convening periodically to review what was done in the last period, and what needs to be done in the next period. The period you choose is up to you, but generally that period should not be longer than every two weeks.

In the next section we're going to look at how we express the work that needs to be done, but as stated in previous chapters we do at a minimum have a scope of work tied back into a specification. At a minimum, you can conceptualise this as an Excel spreadsheet containing a list of things to build. Each project board meeting you look back at what you built and see if it ties up with what you said you'd build. Just this simple reflective process is enough to pretty much guarantee that a project is successful. The reason why we see so many IT project failures is because organisations do not follow that simple principle – just be careful and methodical and structured, and (if the project was ever going to be successful) the project will be successful.

Finally, the size of the team is important as it's important to you want a team effort to get the right input. Moreover, whilst I've been expressing the importance of building a good specification from the start, it's impossible to get a properly complete specification – things will change when it's finally time to pick up the tools and start building, and having the board convened gives everyone – on both your side and the supplier's side – the time and space to ascertain what the reality on the ground is.

Structuring the Work to be Done

The supplier will be responsible for deciding how the work to be done is to be structured. This will align with whatever project management methodology that you and they have agreed will be used to manage the project.

There are broadly two approaches to project management when it comes to software engineering – waterfall and agile. However in 2024, there is a significant bias towards agile over waterfall – which I'll explain as we go.

Both of these approaches have their roots in the principle that we saw back in Chapter 2 in that it is very difficult to describe software before you actually build it. This difficulty is exacerbated by the fact that the engineers who actually build software actually want to get on and do that, and the writing and specifying part is extremely boring to them. Waterfall – the oldest of the approaches – is designed to force a discipline onto people who just want to get on with it. In the waterfall approach, the project goes through several phases, and name comes from the idea that the system "falls down" to the next stage in turn – the analogue being that the process cannot go backwards because water cannot flow uphill.

The steps in waterfall are:

- Gather requirements ("discovery"),
- Design the system,
- Implement the system,
- Test the system,
- Deploy the system,
- Maintain (and ultimately retire) the system.

To come back to the "why" of this, waterfall is a broad attempt to slow down the engineering team so that they actually know what they are trying to build before they start to build it. This encourages proper discovery of the requirements from the customer/end users before the engineering process starts. You may have guessed ahead here and realised that the process we are going through in this book is – from a holistic sense – a waterfall process, in particular we are putting considerable effort into slowing down the discovery and design stages of the project for the simple reason that we want to know with absolute certainty that what we are commissioning is actually what we want.

The problem with waterfall is that it splits the customer interaction into two phases – or more properly, three phases. In the first phase – discovery and design – there is lots of customer interaction, but in the second phase – implementation – there is very little customer interaction. This situation is further exacerbated by the fact that engineers have a tendency to lock themselves in a room and just get on with it and not talk to anyone. On long projects, what historically would happen is that you'd have a long discovery and design phase, and a long implementation phase where for a year or more the engineers would just get on with it, ultimately presenting to the customer something that they did not want because the outputs did not work for them.

The adaptation to this situation was to create an "agile" methodology. There are a number of subdisciplines of agile – which we'll come onto – but in principle they are all the same in that agile breaks a monolithic waterfall process down so that customer interaction happens more frequently. One common approach of agile called "Scrum" uses "sprints", which are short timeboxed periods of usually 2–4 weeks. You start a sprint deciding what you will do, go away and do it, and then reflect on where you got to.

By breaking the project down like this, it's possible to get the outputs in front of the customer more frequently. The customer therefore has more visibility of what is going on and is able to correct problems as they occur as opposed to and of the project where correction is difficult (expensive) or impossible (very expensive).

However, there is a certain tension between fixed price projects and agile, which is why we're looking at the issue here. Agile methodologies are genuinely and generally good for the customer, but they based on the principle that the customer is unable to describe what their requirements are. Agile methodologies are designed for experimentation where the customer has a pot of money to spend, and the vendor thinks that they can get the project delivered for roughly the amount of money the customer wants to spend, for roughly the requirements the customer thinks they have at the outset. We have stressed quick clearly in previous chapters that we want to get a long way away from experimentation, which is why we spent so much time developing a formal specification, a formal scope of works, and a formal timeline. When you're having conversations with the supplier about the agile approach they use, it's important that you do not let this get subverted into a practice whereby the supplier feels they can experiment. You want the strictly structured process of waterfall-esque discovery and design mated to the looser agile process of what gets done in what order.

Agile tends to allow the customer to invent new ideas for implementation during the process – you need to avoid this as you do not want to subvert the fixed-price nature of the project. Any variation from the scope of work that was initially signed off will lead to overruns, and can lead to disputes. (Again, we look at variations in Chapter 9.)

Nowadays, generally all projects are implemented along agile principles but it is important that you control the process and take the good parts of agile and keep the supplier away from even thinking about experimentation. You ultimately do want a waterfall approach to the project (as you effectively cannot have a fixed-price project without a waterfall approach) – and this book is written along waterfall principles – but what you want to do is include the frequent customer touchpoints. As I mentioned above, a common agile methodology called "Scrum" uses 2–4 weeks sprints, and my recommendation is that you run sprints whereby the project board meeting occurs at the end of each sprint. In that meeting you look at what has been done – that is, you actually look and use the outputs the engineers have come up with – and then look at what needs to be done next.

Agile Methodologies Compared

The most common agile methodology is known as "Scrum". It's very likely that your supplier will pitch you on the fact they use an agile methodology, and because Scrum is so common, it's likely to be Scrum that you find governing your project.

The other agile methodologies that we'll sketch out here are Kanban, Lean, Extreme Programming (XP), Crystal, Adaptive Project Framework (APF), and Dynamic Systems Development Methodology (DSDM).

Because software engineers tend to be fast and loose in terms of process, you will likely find that your supplier invents their own methodology by borrowing aspects of different agile methodologies, but also because they are fast and loose will call their invented methodology by a common name. For example, they may say "we do Scrum", only to not do Scrum at all in a purist sense. This doesn't really matter, so long as there is a defined methodology, you understand what it is, and you maintain control over the supplier's delivery process. A "red flag" occurs when the supplier appears to be flexing or changing their methodology from month-to-month – it must be an agreed process that is followed, and a competent supplier will not be changing their methodology midstream.

All of these agile methodologies rely on their being a long-list of work to be done, which is commonly known as the backlog. You will have a long-list like this in your project, because that is what the formal scope of works is. Agile methodologies rely on the customer (with the expert input of the supplier), taking items out of the backlog and giving it to the engineer(s) to do. The customer is then responsible for signing off whether the engineer actually did it – as such, these methodologies give the customer a lot of power. (Although this power is paid off by requiring the customer to be "well behaved" in that they have to be able to stick to the process by attending meetings, taking a time to review outputs, making decisions, etc.)

As mentioned before, Scrum uses sprints to organise its work, but generally all agile approaches use something like sprints, and you can/should align the sprints with the project board meetings. Simply decide in those meetings what work needs to be pulled out of the backlog, as well as checking the work done in the sprint that's coming to a close. When an item is pulled out of the backlog, it becomes a "user story" – which we'll talk about later.

The next word you may hear coming from the supplier is "Kanban". Whilst this is technically a methodology, it is very commonly used to describe a type of artefact called a "Kanban Board". Kanban as a term originated in the Toyota Motor Corporation in the 1940s–50s and Kanban means "visual board". In a Kanban board, you have a list of work on the left that has to go through defined "lanes" ultimately to "fall off" the end of the board on the right. In software engineering those lanes can be things like "Selected for Development", "In Development", "In Testing", or "Waiting Signoff".

Where life can get confusing is that whilst Kanban is an agile methodology, if the supplier uses it, they almost certainly are referring to the artefact of a Kanban Board, rather than the specific agile methodology. As above, this isn't terribly important, just so long as you and the supplier have agreed the approach and that approach does not change.

Coming back to the different methodologies, Kanban and Lean are similar principles in that Toyota invented Kanban as part of their drive towards lean manufacturing. A Lean methodology is designed to reduce waste, and is a collaborative optimising process. It can be used for agile project engineering. Practically, the difference is that Kanban is more visual.

Crystal is designed to be lightweight, and is more applicable for small and medium-sized projects. I would suggest that of the projects that we are discussing in this book, it would be unusual that Crystal is a good fit because of a) the bias to smaller projects, and b) the bias towards flexibility. Being in a fixed-priced project, you do not want flexibility in that sense.

Adaptive Project Framework (APF) has two key features – firstly, like Crystal, it is adaptive. (And again, you don't really want an adaptive approach as adaptive approaches are incompatible with fixed price.) Secondly, it is strongly focused on risk management, and depending on the type of business you are, that may be of interest to you. It does this by baking risk modelling and mitigation steps into the project flow.

Of the last methodology, Dynamic Systems Development Methodology (DSDM) is probably best suited for fixed-price, structured projects of the types described in this book, but it's not commonly used by suppliers. DSDM has a strong focus on value, and prioritises delivery of value early on in the project. Scrum can be somewhat "a la carte", allowing the customer to implement as their fancy takes them, whereas DSDM always has one eye on value delivery. Seeing as the purpose of the endeavour is just to deliver value, this makes a lot of sense. DSDM is also strongly focused on involving stakeholders, again to ensure that any action can be tied through to value. Finally, because of that focus on value, as value is directly affected by cost, there is a natural "pull" within the methodology to ensure that price aligns with value – as you've already decided the price, that natural pull creates a scenario where you're unlikely to overrun on budget.

In summary then, it's ideal to have a supplier that takes an agile approach using a Scrum-like cadence of 2–4 week sprints that tie up with the project board meetings. If you can get them to borrow from DSDM in keeping an eye constantly on the value and the cost, all the better.

Project Management Qualifications

It is possible to gain formal qualifications in project management, however I would suggest that whilst it is a useful data point, I'm not convinced that it should have particular influence on your decision as to which supplier to choose. The day-to-day competence around managing projects is far more important than having representatives at the supplier hold project management qualifications. (In particular there is no guarantee that the supplier representatives on your project board hold the qualifications – it might just be that a senior staff member does.) That said, if you have someone on staff who does have a project management qualification, they likely are a useful addition to the project board so that they can influence the compliance of the rest of the board towards preferring more structure around the project management process.

There are six common project management qualifications, and in the context of this book they're all of approximately equal value: PRINCE2, Project Management Professional (PMP), Certified Associate in Project Management (CAPM), Six Sigma, and two related specifically to agile – Certified Scrum Master (CSM) and Agile Certified Practitioner (ACP).

User Stories

A concept that I particularly like from agile project methodologies is that of "user stories". When a work item is pulled out of the backlog, it can be very helpful to state it as a user story. User stories are much more prosaic than the method we discussed for writing functional specifications back in Chapter 2. When we're defining the project in order to establish a scope and a price, it's important to break down the structure in a way that's compatible with producing those. In particular, by using lots of whitespace, not mushing together sub-requirements, and by using "MUST" and "SHOULD" to allow the user to hone in on what needs to be done or what could be done, it's far easier to create a specification that can be readily "parsed". When it comes time to do the work, what's helpful is being able to check what was specified against what was needed by getting the stakeholder to express in more natural language what they need the system to do.

For example – here's a user story along the lines of the warehouse management piece that we've been looking at so far:

> *"As a warehouse team member, I want to have a visual dashboard that shows real-time inventory levels and order statuses, so that I can prioritise my work and ensure that orders are fulfilled accurately and on time. This dashboard should allow me to quickly identify any inventory shortages or surpluses, and should also display alerts for orders that are at risk of being delayed or not fulfilled. By having this information readily available, I can make data-driven decisions and ensure that our customers receive the best possible service."*

That story is less structured and more natural compared to the manner in which I encouraged you to write the functional specification. That story structure allows the project board and the engineers to get into the mind of the user and understand the "why" that's driving the system implementation directly at the point of implementation. (Remembering of course that the system is being implemented at this point – so if you're a number of sprints into this process, everyone is learning and crafting the system so things are going to change.) Hopefully what should be happening is a close restating of the originally discovered and documented (and priced) requirements, and the user story's contents should not be surprising or astonishing. Of course, it may not be – and if it's not then it's generally good that this has been discovered at this "intention" point as opposed to discover the poor fit after putting effort into implementation.

There are no hard and fast rules about writing stories, except for when we're managing delivery of them, they have to be tied back and have coverage of the specification items in the backlog. For example, the backlog item may have an item along the lines of: *"The warehouse team MUST be able to access a dashboard that shows real-time inventory levels. That table of data MUST have columns for ..."*. A user story is then developed that encapsulated that item in the backlog, along with any others. Ideally a user story should cover more than 2–3 days of implementation and no less than 0.5 days, and you'll need to rely on the supplier to split and combine stories into manageable chunks.

Whilst there are no hard and fast rules, there are some accepted guidelines around what they look like. They should be:

■ Written from the perspective of the end user,
■ Written in simple, non-technical language,
■ Should stand alone – that is, you're not trying to create a complex "mesh" of user stories, try and split them out so that they can be considered and implemented in isolation,

- Should be testable – or more properly, by tying them back to items in the functional specification, they become testable because everything in the functional specification should itself be testable,
- Should be tied back into value – borrowing from our discussion on DSDM, by tying user stories back into the value to the business, you can create an inflexion point where everything done pursuant to the project must deliver value,
- Should not be too granular—they are designed to create context for and act as a check to the items in the functional specification.

Keeping Artefacts

It's important to keep a structured record of the artefacts that come out of the project management and supervision process, even if the project comes under pressure.

All businesses have some way of storing company documents. Nowadays this is often done in the cloud, ideally on SharePoint or a Google Workspace-provided Google Drive instance, but sometimes on Dropbox. Some companies also use traditional on-premises file server. Regardless, there should be one folder where all the project artefacts are kept. Most businesses tend to be good at backing up their files, but it's important that you ask your IT provider to ensure that the files are being properly backed up. The only valuable reason why you ever need to go back and look at these files is if you are in dispute – it would be disastrous to go back to find them only to discover they were gone and there was no backup.

Like all formal meetings, minutes should be kept of project board meetings. The purpose of minutes, as has been the case for all of time, is that people only need to refer to them if something has gone wrong. As you well know by now, one of the themes of this book is to be able to deal with disputes when they occur, and the better the documentation is, the more contained that dispute tends to be. (Disputes get out of hand when people can't agree and have to fish around looking for evidence to support one theory after another.) Minutes for project board meetings should seek to deliver a formal signoff of the work that was done in the previous sprint, and agreement of what is to be done in the next sprint, along with gathering all the various utterances and learns from the meeting that might inform how the next sprint should proceed. Of course, project board meetings should provide a venue for risk containment and accountability, and there's an obvious benefit for minuting these items when they do come up.

The minutes should be stored in the project network/cloud folder as above.

With the increased appetite for using video conferencing services post-COVID, there are risks and opportunities here. One thing that can happen when the project comes under pressure is that suppliers will invite people to "jump on Teams" or "jump on Zoom" to quickly resolve issues. If anything, minuting these meetings are more important than minuting the formal project board meetings as if there are a lot of ad hoc meetings happening, this is a red flag something is going wrong and you likely want to get tighter in terms of oversight here than looser. If ad hoc meetings like this are happening, they must be summarised in email and those emails tracked in the project network/cloud folder.

If you are using video conferencing services, but thanks to systems like Chat-GPT, it's looking like it will become far easier to automatically transcribe and summarise video meetings. To put it another way, it's likely that we'll start to see Microsoft Teams and tools like them create minutes for you. You should take advantage of this, but ensure the generated minutes say what you want them to.

Finally on this topic, be wary of messaging systems that cannot be tracked and captured. An in-person or video conference can be minuted. Emails and attachments can be filed. Instant messaging systems like Microsoft Teams or Slack can be archived, but people tend not to collate these usefully. WhatsApp effectively cannot be automatically archived. Setting up a project group on WhatsApp (even if it's just for internal use), represents poor practice in terms of compliance as the record of what is being said (i.e. the decisions that are being made or the risks that are being surfaces) is ether straightfor-wardly ephemeral or too distant from the rest of the project discussion. However, these systems still can have an impact in legal disputes as anything written down can be presented to a court in support of a case. Try to avoid using systems like this.

Summary

If the project isn't managed, the project will fail. Simply, the more invested the stakeholders are in keeping their hand on the tiller and steering the project, the more successful the project will be. However, in terms of the projects were talking about in this book, we're looking more at supervising the project, rather than directly managing the project – it's down to the supplier to do this active management part. In this approach, the project board is critical, the composition of which needs to blend organisational and supplier representatives. By framing the supplier's role as con-tributing to the joint success of the project, the project board can effectively collaborate and address technical queries promptly.

In the chapter we looked at the difference between waterfall and agile methodologies. These days, practically all projects have an agile feel, as it's so unusual for a supplier just to dis-appear off and develop the solution without coming back for frequent feedback from the customer. There's a tension though in that agile isn't perfectly aligned with the needs of fixed price projects, because fixed price projects tend to drive thinking towards having everything structured and defined up-front.

In conclusion, effective project management, close supervision, and a well-structured approach are crucial for successful project delivery. By adhering to a defined methodology, maintaining regular touchpoints, and aligning customer requirements with implementation, projects have a higher likelihood of meeting their goals.

Chapter 7

Resourcing

Your new IT system will not just spring into existence, unbidden and created by magical forces. Some human beings, you included, will need to sit down and craft it. In this chapter, we'll look at how to optimise the resourcing around project delivery.

External Resourcing

The project that you're undertaking is an outsourced project, and there's an assumption this comes with an outsourced arrangement that you are creating a "done for you" situation where the supplier is building the system for you. This is the exact opposite of how you should be conceptualising the relationship because "done for you" customer/supplier arrangements put too much power in the hands of the supplier. You're not "buying something from them", they are "providing something to you". A better way of conceiving the project is that the company you've chosen to do the work is a delivery partner of your organisation. This approach allows you to say firmly in the driving seat – *your organisation* should look to maintain a leadership position over the project.

DOI: 10.4324/9781003427766-7

This distinction may seem artificial, but it's important, and it may be something that is hard to achieve as you start working together. It is very much an issue of mindset, and it talks about how it is important that the person who is charge of the project at your organisation is an effective leader. The classical distinction between a "leader" and a "manager" is the idea that a "manager" is more of a "boss" who stands between their team and tries to herd them in the direction they should go, there as a leader is an individual who goes where the team needs to go and provides an environment where the team feels like it wants to follow them.

Whilst this distinction is important in business and is regarded as being emerging best practice around leadership, it's especially important with outsourcing relationships because suppliers always have their own imperatives and pressures which can have an adverse effect on your own delivery and project health. By far the most common issue that I've seen feels like a "bait and switch" in that the very good people you've spent ages getting to know and learn how to work with suddenly disappear from the project, although when this happens it is almost always a Hanlon's Razor-type issue. (If you're unfamiliar with the term, Hanlon's Razor says, "Never attribute to malice what can be adequately explained by stupidity".)

This is one of the reasons why in Chapter 4, we discussed the idea of having the engineers who will be doing the work actually attend the presales interviews. The idea here was to start to get the supplier to think that the project is about the people who are doing the project, rather than just being like every other project in their timeline. Ultimately it is down to the supplier to decide how to allocate its resources, although continuing to assign staff that have already spent time in the business tends to be – from their perspective – the option that has less friction. The nightmare scenario is when the resources that have done 80–90% of work on the project suddenly disappear. This often is a red flag that you are in a conflict with the supplier, or you are very shortly about to be in conflict with a supplier, as a supplier will often do this when they detect a falling away of profitability on the project or relationship. For example, let's say that you happen to have their best engineer on your project. Over time, the project has gone OK, but not great, and the supplier realises that long-term from your organisation they might make some money from you, but not as much as they thought they would at the outset. They then get a new opportunity where they think they will make a tonne of money – so they reallocate that great engineer over to this great opportunity.

Your project may well still be OK – but now the situation has got a bit bumpy. You should, wherever possible, try to limit resource changes on your project. There are some situations where this isn't possible (parental leave, the resource actually leaving the supplier, illness, etc.), but from your leadership position, do what you can to set the culture of the project up so that the team is consistent. You can't harangue the supplier about providing the same resources – after all, one of the things that we give up when outsourcing a project is direct control over the minutiae – but it is worth creating a subtle "pressure" that changing resources is "not OK".

There is a related problem here in that you can have time to reallocate and not know about it. For example, an engineer who might be working five days a week on your project may get silently redeployed so that they are now only working three or two. You can detect these problems by examining the project timelines in the meetings. Even a drop of a day a week is 20%, and it's almost always possible to detect a stealthy drop in resource allocation – most people don't detect it because they are not looking, that is, they are not maintaining sufficient oversight over the progress of the project. Maintain the level of oversight that we went through in Chapter 6 and you should detect this problem

A Quick Word about Hiring Staff from the Supplier

Most contracts will have a clause preventing poaching of staff, and usually this clause is bidirectional. I mention this because

I've seen a number of disasters averted by having the customer hire a member of staff who worked with their supplier. What happens though is that because these clauses generally exist, and because there is an expectation that it's bad form, people don't even ask about the process of seconding staff, even though it's a such a highly effective remedial measure. In reality, if someone is going to leave, they're going to leave – all that's happening here is that the customer is removing some of the friction around the process.

Something I've seen work has been for the customer to take the engineer on on a short-term contract. (In this particular scenario, the engineer hated their manager and wanted to leave the supplier, but the engineer was key to the project. Having the engineer move to the customer, and get a very decent day rate, ultimately made everyone happy.)

If you do this, it's critical to get a separate agreement in writing.

Internal Resourcing

Similar to the trope that we just discussed about external resourcing, internal resourcing issues can also fall into the same trap in that we assume that because we have an outsourced relationship, we don't need to worry about internal resourcing. The opposite is true, for the reason that we are working to build a joint team by combining resources from our team and the supplier's team.

There are two types of "pull" on time for the organisation's internal resources – day-to-day requirements, and requirements related to project oversight.

Day-to-Day Resourcing

Ever since Chapter 2 when we went through how to write a specification, I've been looking to encourage a certain optimism in how complete and accurate a functional specification

can be. A lot of the content in Chapter 6 on alludes to the idea
that it's not really possible to build a specification and then
build the solution from that without having to make adjustments as you go. Where the "rubber meets the road" as it were
is when the actual engineer is physically building the solution –
and it's certainly possible for queries to come up during this
process. This manifests itself in the engineer needing information from people in the business.

It's very important to get to a position where the organisation is able to respond to these requests effectively and without
delay. The reason for this is that if queries should be coming up
in the project planning meeting, and we should have enough
discipline over the design of the work so that queries are
squished out of the process ahead of time. If a query is coming
up that requires immediate satisfaction, it by definition has to be
a "blocking" item – that is, one that is preventing the engineer
from making progress. An engineer who can't do their work
generates two problems. Firstly, by definition it is creating a
delay in the project – any time the engineer is waiting for a
response to their query is time that will at a minimum get tacked
directly on to the end of the project timeline. (In reality it can be
much worse where a domino effect can cause more slippage.)
Secondly, any time the engineer is sitting around, from the
supplier's perspective, that will directly erode their margin. Much
as this book is "all about you", part of managing the relationship
through to a point where it is a genuinely beneficial delivery-
focused long-term relationship is ensuring that both sides get
enough value from that relationship and (from their perspective)
being frustrating to work with won't help that.

What is required then is that the organisation is able to field
queries in a rapid and responsive fashion. This is going to be
down to you as leadership within the organisation. The main
pushback you will receive aligns with what we learned about in
the last chapter about Type A activities and Type B activities. To
recap, Type A activities are those that are directly aligned to the

general mission of the organisation – for example, the warehouse manager would regard "receiving goods into the warehouse" as core mission. Type B activities are hygiene factors that the business needs to do, one class of hygiene factor being the introduction of a new IT system. From my experience, we see a continuum of behaviour from people who love Type B activities, and those who abhor Type B activities.

In this particular issue of needing immediate resolution of issues that pop up out of nowhere, and need clarification if the person who ultimately knows the answer enjoys Type B activities, there's a solid chance the query will be resolved quickly. However, if the person does not enjoy Type B activities, this often creates a blockage. Moreover – much like when you're driving and a rabbit runs out in front of your car you should immediately think "is there another one coming?" – when you do see a blocking problem like this, there are usually more problems, which are related, coming down the line. As such, blocking problems can become politically entangled. This is why it's important that organisational leadership (not just project leadership) is involved. Leadership needs to say to those within the organisation that when the engineers do have queries, it's an organisational priority to resolve those queries smoothly or quickly. It's essential to structure things so that the organisation gets out of the way to respond rapidly to queries from the supplier that are blocking the project.

Oversight Resourcing

Again calling back to the last chapter, the oversight resources are primarily those resources that are allocated to the project board. Like the discussion above, you should structure the board to prefer those who enjoy Type B activities, but who also have some skill at managing projects.

However, there are two more types of oversight resources that are important to the business, which are those that are set-up as checks and balances to make sure the organisation is being sensible. I suggest that people do this on the principle that the only thing that is worse than being wrong is finding out that you were wrong having spent a lot of money on the privilege.

An easy way to do this is to socialise the work being done within the organisation. You can do this formally or informally – although it's again because (a) IT is boring and (b) some people don't like being taken away from their Type A activities, if you can find a way to do this informally this tends to yield better results.

Way back in the day it used to be very common for there to be "user groups" – self-organised groups of users who would come together and try to work out how best to use a piece of software within their businesses. Once vendors worked out that user groups were happening, vendors used to get involved, and the whole set-up worked nicely. People don't tend to do this anymore – although they really should. (For example, would it not be helpful for a collection of midmarket manufacturing businesses to meet up and discuss how their SAP Business One implementations were working, along with representatives of SAP to provide some steer and head-off problems?) What I would encourage is that the business sets-up a user group for the new system and makes it easy for people to get their hands on and provide feedback very early on in the process.

You will need a balance here because you have designed what you want to deliver, and that whole process is relatively brittle. (You've agreed the deliverables, the price, and the timeline.) Feedback is incredibly valuable, but any "just one thought" that anyone in that room has the potential to derail the project. Ideally, you've done such a good job of distilling the organisation's needs into the design that all that's happening in that room is validation. There will be things that come up that would be genuinely helpful, but you and the project team will have to assess whether it's a valuable variation for that "v1" release, or whether that will be coming in "v2". What you are really looking for is any sign that the project has a serious problem that will derail it – we talk about project failure in Chapter 11.

Board Resourcing

When I was planning this chapter and going through my notes, there was an emerging realisation that was so surprising to me, I had to spend some time in my local Starbucks making an inventory to make sure my observation was accurate. That observation is this: *in 100% of the situations where I have been called in to advise on an IT systems project failure, the board were completely unaware of the failure until it slapped them in the face.*

Or, to put it another way, the board is always caught off-guard by IT project failure.

Over in the UK, the police developed something called "The System of Car Control", which is a systematic approach to driving. The principle of The System of Car Control is that if you follow the system – that is, you adhere to the process – crashing a motor vehicle becomes impossible. It does this by making an assumption that it is possible to gather 100% of the information pertaining to the vehicle's travel, 100% of the information pertaining to the environment, and then processing that information with 100% efficiency to anticipate and ameliorate every risk.

It does rather ignore the human factor, but regardless my observation is that the reason why the board is always caught off-guard is because they are not receiving 100% of the information related to the project. If the board knows about the issue and still drives the car into the wall – that's on them.

Why then does the board not receive the information that they need? In my experience, this is usually some variation of a lack of interest in the project and/or an overreliance on the person who is tasked with reporting into the board. This ironically gets bad when the person on the board is well-liked and trusted as the board just assumes that person knows what they are doing. I have seen just one occasion where the person reporting into the board was just outright lying – and in this instance the person just kept kicking the can down the road in fear of losing their job.

In fairness, what the board needs in order to be a legitimately valuable ally in making sure the project delivers is data. That data also needs to be simple. Given the structure as to how we propose running the project in this, we're in good shape for this in that all we have to do is give the board sight of the project progress. That data will reveal if the project is slipping – and it's the slippage is the ultimately metric of project health. Ultimately though, signing yourself up to invite oversight and challenge by the board is a critical check and balance to maintaining a low level of risk in the project.

Communication

We tend to divide the skills we need to do our jobs into soft skills and hard skills. My own personal philosophy is that it's generally hard to fit human behaviour into little boxes and that everything we humans tends to do is always more naturally expressible on a continuum. Soft and hard skills I believe comes from a sort of Mad Men era – or even one a bit older – that is, a time when hard skills were literally "it's 'hard' because it involves smacking a hammer into a piece of metal", and anything else we did was unworthy. As I'm writing this, we're in something of a renaissance of coming to realise that the place where we work should be filled with kind people treating each other kindly, that actually its not cool to bully your way to the top, that people have lives and being able to fit (good) work in around complex personal lives is the way to go, etc.

This isn't a book about leadership or culture, but I have a motto that I will share in case you like it: "Everyone is doing their best with what they've got".

The problem with dividing skills into soft and hard is that it comes with the baggage that the hard skills are the important ones and the soft skills have to fit in around it. The most damaging aspect of this is that businesses tend to lump "communication" in as a soft skill, with the implication that it's not important. The reality is that communication is the most important skill. Business is a team sport. The reason why people **organise** themselves into **organisations** is because of the gestalt effect of the sum of the parts being greater than the whole. Being a fan of etymology and playing with words, I like to then jump from **organisation** to **organism**, and hopefully it's not then stretching the analogy to liken communication to a nervous system. You can't do anything without communication. Yes, individuals need to be able to contribute, but even Michael Jordan couldn't have done what he did just on raw talent. He became the greatest sportsperson ever because he was able to play in a team, and that team communicated.

Again, this is not a culture or leadership book, but it's so absolutely critical that you foster at a minimum *fantastic* communication between everyone involved in project delivery. I labour this point because in an IT systems project, there are aspects to this that are like pushing water uphill. Technical engineers like to get their heads down and get on with the job, but in that mode they are not asking end users if the solution fits. End users tend to find IT systems boring and complicated, and will often not want to put their hands up and admit they don't know how to operate the systems they are presented with, meaning that feedback is clipped. We saw about how boards often don't know a project is flying headfirst into a mountain just because no one told them. You will get better outcomes with better communication. You should do whatever you can to make what hopefully starts as a baseline "good" communication into something fantastic.

Dealing with "Blips" in Availability

Certainly for the next 50 years, to actually build our software systems we will need to use humans, and humans can't always be in the office/at work when you need them to be. (This is also the same as machinery – plant breaks down too.) From time-to-time, we'll have to deal with "blips" in the availability of resources. Whatever resource this is can either have their workload reassigned, or a blockage will be created.

For the external resourcing, the reality is that for the scale of projects that we're talking about in this book, that resource is effectively irreplaceable when we look at short-term absences. The principle is behind this is something we'll look at in Chapter 9, but the principle is that if you have someone who is, for example, working on a three-day-long story on the warehousing module, they do one day and then go off sick for a week with "flu", it makes more sense to wait them to come back and finish it as it'll take someone new a day to get up-to-speed on the work. (Non-technical staff usually hugely underestimate the time taken to switch tasks.) Effectively this becomes an exercise to plan in the lost time – but to reiterate the key is that on these little "micro-absences", you should roll with the punches as opposed to try and transfer the work.

For longer-term absences unexpected for external resources, the work should be transferred. (Longer-term expected absences, which can be short such as a holiday, or longer such as parental leave, this should have already been planned in.) To transfer the work, the project board will need to agree the strategy, but effectively this will just be a shorter, ad hoc version of work that's already been done to plan in the timeline. It is likely that work will be re-sequenced.

Like the issue related to short-term absence above, time lost to picking up someone else's work is often considerably underestimated, so it's beneficial to reduce churn.

Absences in internal resources work in a similar way. As above, internal resources only block if they are a unique source of information, for example, they know something specific about an operational/domain area of the business and they are the only one who knows it well enough to express it in a way that aligns with shaping the final system outcome. For short-term absences, it is likely better to wait for them to return. For longer-term absences, you have two problems, one internal to you, and one related to the project – the organisation will naturally have to fill that knowledge gap anyway. This will almost always naturally lead to re-sequencing.

Project board members should not end up as a blocking resource as they sit above and supervise. There may be some reasons why the board is unable to sign-off a decision. That then becomes a business continuity issue. If you look outside of this issue, another way to look at it is that you have a "committee" within the business that is able to get itself stuck, and that generally shouldn't be.

Managing Geographically Dispersed Teams

It's possible that the team you are working with is geographically as this model of working is very common in IT systems development. If you're working with a geographically dispersed team, here are some things to consider:

1. Use the right communication tools: Communication is key in managing dispersed teams. Make sure to use communication tools like video conferencing, instant messaging, email, and project management software to keep everyone on the same page.
2. Set clear expectations: It is important to set clear expectations for work hours, deadlines, and communication protocols to ensure that everyone is on the same

page. Make sure to communicate this to your team and ensure that everyone is following the same guidelines.

3. Build a culture of trust: Trust is critical when managing dispersed teams. Foster a culture of trust by being transparent, responsive, and supportive. Encourage open communication and be available to answer questions or provide guidance as needed.

4. Provide regular feedback: Regular feedback is important for both personal and team development. Schedule regular check-ins with each team member to provide feedback on their work and identify areas for improvement.

5. Celebrate successes: Celebrate team successes, no matter how small. This will help to build morale and foster a sense of community among team members who may not work in the same physical location.

6. Encourage team building: Encourage team building activities such as virtual social events, team lunches, or online games to help build relationships and foster collaboration.

In summary though, the first item re-communication is essential (a point I laboured earlier), the others are nice to have, but remain important.

Fractional Support and IT Leadership

This book is principally looking to help businesses that don't have an in-house IT leadership function. It should be said that projects go much better if you do have someone on staff who knows how to do all this. I do this sort of thing for a living, and the idea of this book is that if someone wanted to go and download the part of my brain that would teach a management team how to buy a complex IT system without my direct support, this is what I would say.

One of the things I have observed over my career – and this has got somewhat more entrenched over the past ten years or so – is that businesses grow their senior leadership in a way that the IT person is offered a set at the table last. A board will tend to start with one or two founders – one of those will be the CEO, and one will be aligned to a job that fits their career. In a technical business that is delivery-focused, this will be a delivery role, for example, Chief Operating Officer (COO). In a business that is sales-focused, this might be a Chief Marketing Officer (CMO) or Chief Revenue Officer (CRO). The next hire tends to be whichever one of those is missing – so if there's a COO, a CMO or CRO would be added next; if there's a CMO or CRO, a COO will be added next.

The next hire tends to be a Chief Financial Officer (CFO). You then might think about a Chief Human Resources Offer (CHRO). What comes in late is this technology role, which is typically a Chief Information Officer (CIO) or a Chief Technology Officer (CTO). The fact there are two common roles that seem to be exactly the same speaks volumes about the cultural preference for obfuscation in the IT industry ... The difference is that CIOs tend to look inwards towards operational imperatives, and CTOs tend to look outwards towards customer imperatives. To illustrate, if given an option to implement an ERP system or an app for customers to self-service their own orders, a CIO will prefer to do the ERP first, the CTO will prefer to do the app first.

That in itself is an important point because both the ERP and the app should be built, because holistically within a broad IT strategy, both should exists and both should interoperate and interconnect. It's this concept of "strategy" that is omitted from the IT play within midmarket organisations that have not yet made that investment in a CIO or CTO.

Strategy is everything, and it's curious to me that most businesses understand the need for strategy across these operational areas of the business, but rarely address the absence of strategy around information technology. By way of illustration, if you ask the "person on the street" what a CFO does, most of them will look at you and answer that they are a "fancy and/or senior accountant". In reality, a CFO spends most of their days working on strategic initiatives to ensure the business continuously improves its financial governance. Very little of a CFO's job involves keying in someone's Starbucks receipts into Xero. (Hopefully the organisation's CIO/CTO has managed to get a more appropriate accounting system for a midmarket business – but avoiding having the wrong systems for the job at hand is part of what a CIO/CTO does.) Senior staff tend to know that a CFO is more than just a fancy accountant, but this blind spot in my experience is fairly universal in midmarket businesses. The reason why I say that this is what I think happens at the senior level – senior leadership tends not to know what a senior IT leader does, and struggles to conceptualise the value that having IT leadership and strategy brings, and as a result does not prioritise bringing those skills into the business.

If it's helpful, these are the types of things that a CIO/CTO does:

- **IT strategy** – listening to what the business needs and building out the systems to support it,
- **Digital transformation** – discovery and implementation of initiatives that help the business reduce operational friction and improve the customer experience,
- **Infrastructure** – ensuring the organisation has the physical tools needed for its digital work,
- **Cybersecurity** – hardening the organisation against cybersecurity attacks (malware, phishing, rogue employees),
- **Cloud** – migrating workloads to modern cloud-based solutions,
- **Governance** – ensuring the organisation is meeting its regulatory and ethical goals,

- **Vendor management** – keeping the relationships with the organisation's IT vendors heathy,
- **Budgeting** – maintaining control over the IT spend,
- **Business continuity** – ensuring the organisation can remain operational in the event of a disaster,
- **IT project management** – implementing projects, much like the type of project that we're discussing in this book.

Chief "anythings" are expensive, and a common way to fix the problem now to is to hire a "fractional" version of whatever executive you want. "Fractional" is a truly horrible name, but we seem to be stuck with it. Essentially it means "part-time" or "consulting". If you don't need a 40-hour-a-week CxO, you might be OK with paying someone a day rate for part-time involvement. I work as a Fractional CTO, and having spent some time looking at how people buy this, they do it in two ways – ask someone in your network (as we did to build the suppliers long-list in Chapter 4), or use LinkedIn.

This book isn't about IT strategy, or the need to have IT leadership within the organisation, but every organisation can benefit from it.

Summary

If you're trying to build a project, it's obviously important that you have someone who can do the actual work. Resourcing a project though does absolutely does need to be a two-sided, win-win arrangement. A very common way for projects to fail is that the customer does is not able to utilise its stakeholders properly. Sudden disappearance of key personnel mid-project is another very common way in which resourcing can adversely affect projects. A good way to deal with this is to set an expectation early on (even pre-sale) that certain engineers have to stick around for the life of the project.

We also saw that it's of critical importance that people who are able to resolve queries and issues that arise during project are highly available to the project. We also learnt about the significance of oversight resourcing, including project board members and checks and balances to ensure sensible decision-making.

Chapter 8

Special Considerations for Bespoke Software

Spend more than five minutes with me in person, and I'll happily tell you that I learnt to write computer software when was 8 years old. Now, a good number of years later, I continue to write software every day. My first love is software. If you sequence my DNA and this was even vaguely possible, you'd see the words "BESPOKE SOFTWARE" written in my genes.

For me, there is no more appropriate application of bespoke software than within business. However, in 2024, established companies rarely buy bespoke software.

To qualify that, within the types of projects discussed in this book, the implementation aspect is always bespoke. The core system that you buy will not be bespoke – as we learnt earlier this is commercial of-the-shelf (COTS) software.

I've included a chapter in this book for two reasons – firstly, some businesses will know they want to buy some bespoke software, and the manner in which you engage with that process is different to the process we've discussed so far. Secondly, it's worth knowing *why* bespoke software is often a great fit for organisations. Leadership teams often have blind spots around the value that it can provide.

DOI: 10.4324/9781003427766-8

Why Use Bespoke Software?

Go back far enough in history, and there was no commercial off-the-shelf software. Effectively, every piece of software that an organisation needed had to be written from scratch as bespoke solutions. Because some people in software companies under-stand business opportunities, over time the value that was in those bespoke solutions began to get packaged up. Typically this followed a "vertical" pattern, in that a company might hit upon the idea of building a piece of software for managing doctors surgeries, or gyms, or garages, or video rental stores and then packaging it up so that it could be sold. Again if you go back far enough, software was literally sold "off the shelf", with computer stores having physical boxes containing manuals and disks. The first job I ever had was working in a computer shop, and behind the counter we would have shelves of software that people would buy for their businesses. (There is a YouTuber over here in the UK who has recreated a UK computer shop from the 1980s and you can go and visit it ...)

For a while, there was a balance whereby there was sort of a parity in price to performance between the COTS solutions and bespoke solutions. If a business wanted some software to manage its warehouse, it was possible to write business cases both for buying and implementing a COTS solution, or com-missioning a fully bespoke system.

Today though, you'd have to be quite brave to commission a bespoke solution from a well-served off-the-shelf market. For example, if you have a chain of dental practices, you would have to go a long way to argue that it was better to build your own system for managing that business compared to buying an off-the-shelf practice management system.

The mistake that organisations make now rather inverts the situation in that management doesn't go any further than im-plementing the COTS solution, and this is a huge mistake in terms of missed opportunities.

Regardless of what your organisation does, there is one truism about what the organisation *is*. Your organisation is utterly unique. The way the pieces of your organisation fits together, the customers you have, the people you have, and the constellation of organisations that support it all create an entirely unique entity.

The principle of a COTS solution is that it has a broad enough feature set to do anything that your organisation needs it to do through customisation. All you have to do is decide which features you want to use, fit them/customise them to the organisation's uniqueness, and ignore anything you don't want to use (hopefully managing to avoid paying for the parts you don't need).

This approach provides the features you need within each piece of software you have, but what is missing – and what people stop short of – are the parts which are so unique to you, no software vendor is ever going to provide a solution on spec. This falls into two camps – (a) the unique combination of systems and people that is you and (b) the stuff that only you can do.

Integration, particularly integrations about data, is the first part where businesses fall down. (We're going to talk about data separately.) I'm not sure what to attribute this to, but over the past 5–10 years there has been a kind of "falling away" of appetite to closely integrate within midmarket businesses. You should do what you can to closely integrate systems together.

When systems are implemented with a business, each one will have its own store of data. By default, those systems do not share data – each one contains just the data it needs to do its job, but because systems cannot magic up data out of thin air, that data has to be presented ("inputted") into the system in some way. Data also doesn't exist just for its own sake – data represents some thing in the real world. This is called "modelling". For example, in the accounts system there will be a record that represents a customer – i.e. the record of the customer in the accounts system "models" the customer in the real world.

This process continues down to each and every aspect in the building. There will be data that models every employee, data that models every invoice, every order, every palette in the warehouse (and every warehouse), every box on every palette, every computer, every printer, every bank account, and so on and so on. This means that if you look at all your computer systems and are able to determine that every real-world thing, across that constellation of computer systems there exists an exact point-in-time model of your business. If you store a universal set of historical information, it's not just a "point-in-time" model, that model can be used to go back and describe the exact state of the business at any time. You can also go the other way and, with the right know-how, project that model into the future in order to make projections of what the model of the business would look like at any point in the future.

This is a very ideal state. The inherent challenge within this is that each system wants to stores its own data that is both (a) potentially duplicated between systems, and (b) does not "flow" between systems unless it is made to do so. For example, for a given customer – e.g. a supermarket that is buying your products, that customer is modelled in the accounting system, the CRM system, and in an informal/instructed way in emails and phone records, i.e. there is duplication. The customer journey through your business demands that they touch multiple systems, but that one single instance of a customer may be represented multiple times in the overall model, and as they pass from one stage of the journey to the next (which may involve them flip-flopping between different stages by design), they will take data and change data as they go through that journey. If that data cannot flow between systems (because of the duplication and/or lack of integration), two things happen. You either (a) cannot create an excellent, frictionless, continually improving experience for the customer, or (b) you can create an excellent, frictionless, continually improving experience for the customer, but you have an absolute mess of inefficiency, breakdown, and burnout suffered by staff behind the scenes.

An in-house IT leader will naturally try and smoothly shape a single consistent model that both represents and runs across the whole business. They will not necessarily try to do this with a conscious intent, it just naturally happens as a result of best practice because that practice by default (a) prefers one representation of something in the model as opposed to duplication, and (b) prefers smooth flow of data between disparate systems through closer integration. If you are a midmarket business with no in-house IT leadership, this is the sort of capability gap that will ultimately need addressing because modern end-customers (whether B2C or B2B) demand that more and more "friction" is removed from their customer experience. This is only practicable through an IT systems-based approach.

Without having in-house IT leadership, the fruit that is both low-hanging (i.e. easy to get) and reachable (i.e. possible to get) is that of integration. The reality is that all businesses must integrate the system, and by default will resort to a manual integration. (For example, if you onboard a new customer, they'll both be in any operational systems you need to deliver the value, and in your accounting system. It's not uncommon to double-key the customer details into the accounts system.) What I'm proposing is that you look at a technical/automated integration between the systems. This is half the battle. The other half is that of attitude and philosophy, which we will look at now.

A Worked Example: "Revenue Operations (RevOps)"

There is an emerging subculture, particularly within US-based software businesses at the moment for something called "RevOps", which is short for "revenue operations". To me, this

is the single most powerful "technical philosophy" that organisations can use to improve the customer journey, without
mincing staff through overwork and burnout in the process.
The purpose of it is to make the experience the customer has
within your organisation throughout their life "slicker" from
initial awareness and interest through to eventual retirement.

The phrase finds its roots in a now common subculture
within software businesses called "DevOps". The problem
DevOps solves is that the process of actually building the
software ("development", which we've tended to call "engineering" in this book) and the process of actually running the
software ("operations") are very different disciplines, but for the
business to get value out of the investment it makes in developing the software, both have to work together. By way of an
analogy, marketing and sales are very different disciplines, but
have to work together – without marketing, sales has no leads;
without sales, marketing has nowhere to put leads.

The principles of DevOps is that developers need to know a
little bit more about the day-to-day work of operations, so that
the decisions they make are "sympatico" with what the operations team needs to do their day-to-day work. The same is true in
reverse. Oftentimes you'll need someone in the role of inter-
locutor/arbitrator between the two to make things run smoothly.
To illustrate with semi tongue-in-cheek example, the development team may build some software that requires massive, expensive servers to run on, and the operations team may in turn
indicate that those are too expensive and there is no budget. The
truth might be that the development teams need to find an
approach that requires less computing horsepower, and the
operations team may need to find some more budget.

RevOps looks to integrate the sales, marketing, and the
customer success teams. I love the term "customer success" as
it's so nicely customer-focused. This is what you could call the
"operations" team, i.e. the team that actually gets the value
delivered to the customer, whatever that happens to be.

("Customer success" has a slightly different meaning in software-as-a-service businesses as customers for those sorts of businesses tend to be a combination of both skittish and at arms-length, but I still like the term for any business.) I also like to broaden out RevOps to include the purely financial aspects of the business, particularly around cashflow. Organisations should broadly do what they can to get better at reducing friction around cash coming in, and better add adding a bit of friction around cash flowing out.

RevOps absolutely is something that can be applied to any business, and a lot of it can be done with philosophy, although it ultimately will require strong IT leadership making and IT investment. But for now, we can look at some of that lower-hanging fruit.

One simple thing that most midmarket businesses can do is start to collect payments using methods other than bank transfer, e.g. Direct Debit in the UK or Automated Clearing House (ACH) in the US, or by broadening out card payment support. This fits into a RevOps philosophy of preferring to reduce friction in bringing cash in. However, there's a friction point here in that you might want customers to set up Direct Debit/ACH, but if that process is difficult to do, you might not get people signing up to that process. One option is that you can automate emails out to a customer during onboarding seeking to get them to click through a link and go through a neat little process to get their Direct Debit/ACH authorised. That itself will have a potential friction point in that if that customer cancels their authority, what do you do?

This is where you start to get into a "turtles all the way down" aspect of RevOps, although that's not in and of itself bad – everything is an opportunity. Continuing the example, you need to be able to detect the authority has gone away, and action it. One option is that the accounts team notices it, emails the account manager, and the account manager looks to raise the customer on the phone. But that's quite high friction in terms of the internal operations, plus you have an issue here as a customer cancelling an authority can either (a) happen by accident, or (b) be an indicator that you are about to lose the customer, i.e. you have a retention problem. Either way, you have to action it. Does that action involve, for example, putting a task in the CRM so that the account manager can escalate the issue. Then, what happens if the account manager is away for two weeks, by which time that annoyed customer is getting overly fond of a competitor? You need a way for other staff to pick up the slack – this talks to the way that tasks are managed and flowed through the CRM system as part of that customer success function. A RevOps approach means iterating small continuous improvements, albeit you also need a culture where it's possible to continually track and discover where those improvements can be made.

You can see there how even a small decision – in this case, enable Direct Debit/AHC – has this ripple affect across the accounts, sales, and operations teams, both at the point of onboarding, and at a pinch-point in the customer's life. But it's ultimately beneficial as the organisation is able to work much more in lockstep with the customer. Without enabling Direct Debit/ACH, i.e. without kicking any of this off, and only having the customer able to pay through bank transfer/direct deposit, you're not maintaining friction around bringing cash in (which is not great), but you are losing this "early warning" system around a retention problem.

In this worked example, there is some reasonably sophisticated technical integration and automation user stories, but in reality they would be relatively cheap to introduce and manage. You can do some of this – you can do some of it in quite a "janky" way. When the Direct Debit/ACH provider tells you authority has been cancelled, you can literally just create a rule in Outlook to forward that notification to the sales manager automatically, where they can action that exception manually. You can find and action that sort of win just with the right culture and philosophy – you don't need technical leadership or even a budget to start moving in the right direction.

Your "Secret Sauce"

When I start working with a new business, in my head I start with a blank sheet of paper and design one piece of software that acts as a "business operating system" to that business. What I want to produce is a "single pane of glass" that (a) brings to a single place every piece of data the business needs to access in order to make decisions and (b) provides a single interface to perform the key operations related to the business activities.

This is a very "blue sky ideal" kind of space that is not easily achievable to most businesses – but if we can kick it around a bit and get our heads around why it's beneficial, we can look at some "good enough" examples that are more readily achievable.

This talks to the integration between the systems, as you cannot do this without a deliberate, coherent strategy to link and integrate all of those disparate systems. It also talks about choices regarding implementation of future systems, as those new systems have to be able to fit into this single "operating system" approach. The reason why you do this is so that you can present to the business something that underpins this customer-centric, single-journey idea. Whenever we have a new customer come into the business – and this starts at the point when they are as a potential lead, i.e. before they are contracted – we need to be thinking about what systems they will touch as the organisation delivers value to them. Coming back to this RevOps idea, what we are trying to do is break down the barriers between the various areas of the business and "de-silo" the data that pertains to each customer's experience. It's easier to get everyone on the same page in relation to that if people are used to logging onto one system that *is* the organisation and represents the end-to-end of the experience.

However, as mentioned that "business operating system" is hard to do, but the integration is reasonably straightforward. Once system are integrated, it's possible to go to staff and encourage them to think that across all the systems in the organisation, anything that is modelled only exists once. In computer science, this is called the "single source of truth". From a systems architecture point of you it (effectively) demands that there is only one representation of anything anywhere. The reason why we do this is that duplication is difficult to manage. If a customer gets married and changes their name, it's best to be able to make this change in the CRM and have the (separate) billing system get their correct name out of the CRM.

(There is a small wrinkle to this in that you can be a little less dogmatic in this approach when it comes to the actual accounting systems. Because those systems are required in every business to provide that baseline regulatory oversight, and because they work in a way where data is difficult to undo and unwind, you can get away with duplication. For example, you may put a purchase order in an ERP system, which you ultimately delete because it was not needed. If that PO led to actual purchase transactions that really did happen in the real world, you cannot just delete that PO from the accounts system.)

Given that it's difficult to create this "business operating system", the next best place to concentrate on bespoke software within the business is in building the system that represents the one thing that you do that no one else can do.

Every business will have that one thing that only they can do – the one aspect of the value provision that is completely unique to them, and difficult for other people to do because they have built up value, expertise, and intellectual proper around provision of that value. I call this their "secret sauce".

You should do what you can to express your secret sauce through software. As you are the organisation on the planet that can do that unique, secret sauce-y thing, by default this means you will be building some sort of bespoke solution to do this.

In fairness, it's very common for businesses to develop bespoke solutions for this purpose without a conscious awareness. It's well-known that modern businesses often operate via a set of homegrown Excel files – this is to all intents and purposes a bespoke software system. (Those files hold data and there will usually be some automated logic to change and manipulate data in response to input, and they provide output – that's all software is.) The reason why businesses do this is because a "proper" solution is not available to them. This can be for many reasons, but when it comes to a system to support the secret sauce aspect of the business, there usually is not a solution on the market even if a budget can be found to suit.

There are many reasons why using Excel to operate the business is not a great idea. (Talk to any IT practitioner about using Excel to underpin a core business operation and watch their blood pressure go through the roof.) There are particular problems around scalability (it is difficult to share Excel files effectively between anything other than very small teams), and business continuity (damage or lose the file and that business unit, or even the whole business, cannot trade). The better approach is to invest in a bespoke system that can be properly designed, can properly scale, and is a proper candidate for inclusion into a business continuity plan.

Oftentimes business will create a bespoke system that targets the "special sauce" function by having someone on staff who has enough amateur skills to create such a thing. This usually results in a system that is running on Microsoft Access, or FileMaker, although we are now starting to see systems like this emerge through No Code and Lo Code solutions, especially as tools like Power Apps and Power Automate are included with Microsoft 365. This approach is not automatically bad. Where the risk in this falls is when it falls into "shadow IT", which in this context are IT systems that the business is dependent on, but that the system doesn't know about. Shadow IT almost always creates cybersecurity risk, information security risk, and business continuity risk. They are worth it because these sorts of system *always* have value because they contain an authentic expression of the organisation's operations, crafted by people who (usually) care about the business.

It tends to be better, perhaps ironically that systems like this are built by senior staff. This is because when a system just "evolves" like this, and when it becomes core, you need a senior stakeholder to constrain the risk profile. A co-founder or senior director of the business is less likely to leave, leaving the organisation floundering around trying to find someone to support the business when compared to a junior member of staff who is more likely to leave.

The final risk point for these sorts of solutions is that when the organisation "grows up" and decides it wants something proper, the work that was done in crafting the homegrown system gets chucked out. This is in virtually every case an error. At a minimum what you have in systems like this is a prototype for how a proper "grown-up" system should be working. You should take care to take the learns from that system and bake it into the functional specification for any replacement systems, trimming off the parts that don't work so well and crafting strong "v2" versions of the parts that do work well.

Data

In the world of computer theory, data and systems are equally important. However, as this book is about buying IT systems, there is a slant towards talking more about systems than data.

The reality is that within modern business, it is critical to be able to be able to access and work with data. The way that I like to think about it is that data is like the "clay" that the business must learn to manipulate and mould as if it were a potter throwing that clay on the wheel.

Every activity within the business will produce data, and it's up to the business to learn how to illuminate that data to produce insights. This will require bespoke software development to produce the tools and frameworks that you need to extract and present the data. The value really comes in being able to combine data from other sources, as this is where you tend to get insights.

For example, we spoke before about making systems and process changes with regards to reducing friction in bringing cash into the business. I raise this point because nearly all businesses have close at hand the requisite skills that when focused can do this job of reducing friction. Practically, this might mean getting better at managing the accounts receivable process – i.e. running that report in the accounts system and spending time chasing money coming in.

From a data perspective, is it valuable to be able to be able to mash together accounts receivable data with customer support/operational data? If we do that, we would be able to see which customers are (a) a pain to get money out of and that also (b) cause a lot of noisy operational problems. That's illuminating an insight that's actionable, whatever that action may be, and it happens because the organisation is more open to understanding and working with what data it has, not because any big or complex investment has been made.

Generally, the more systems you have, the more data you have, and the more you develop a culture around being "data first", the more advantages you get from having that data.

We're seeing a shift in the lifetime of that data, however. Previously, IT specialists have tended to take a view that (a) storage is so cheap that it is effectively free, and (b) it's better to have something and not need it as it is to need something and not have it. IT systems have therefore tended to be built on the principle of a killer whale consuming krill – open wide and just capture everything. With a more modern view around data retention and privacy, organisations need active management of data retention. Practically this means that you cannot gather data without a plan as to how you expunge it from the business at an appropriate time.

I will just round this discussion off by talking briefly about AI. I've avoided talking too much about AI in this book because as of the time in writing in 2024, we are seeing at least an emerging awareness that these tools will be disruptive. The capabilities that we are seeing in this tools now will have an impact, but it's much too early to say what. Also I will say that the capabilities of the tools are universally overstated, and the industry itself has a rich history of overstating capabilities so it's almost guaranteed this will continue.

The reason why I've added a part about AI to discussion on data is that AI is purely and simply statistical models around data. What we call AI is really "machine learning". To build an ML system, you provide it with a set of data that is labelled. The classic example of this is spam email classification – you give an ML system a set of data that you say "is spam", and a set of data that you say "is not spam". The ML system will then create a model using that data. Now when you give it an email it's never seen before, it uses that model to guesstimate whether the email should be classified as "spam" or "not spam".

Even ChatGPT is an ML system. The process it goes through is that it produces a word, and then statistically guestimates what the next word is likely to be. It keeps doing that until it produces sentences and paragraphs. It's not thinking, it's not intelligent, it's just an incredibly impressive application of mathematics.

The danger to businesses is that it's easy to think that AI is doing more than it is, and as a result it's easy to buy into "snake oil"-type solutions that seem to be doing something they are not. However, any AI system tracks the quality of the data that it has to work with. The better you are with data, the more disciplined the organisation when it comes to data practice, any AI or AI-like tools that you bring into the business more effective. But it's that way round – the data is the dog, the AI tool is the tail. Don't get bamboozled into a "tail ways the dog"-type situation.

Outsourced Development

The purest form of bespoke software development is outsourced software product development. This is where the organisation seeks an outsourcing arrangement to build a product, for example an app that is to be used by consumers, or a platform that is to be used by business customers or partners/ stakeholders.

There is a huge difference between this sort of bespoke work, and the sort of "bespoke customisation" that this book primarily focuses on. This sort of bespoke work is much more like you sitting down with a blank piece of paper and drawing out a completely unique thing that does not exist anywhere else. If you're customising an ERP system, there are natural limits to that work. Most warehouses look the same – they are big boxy buildings with shelves and you put things on the shelves. You may have something exotic like said warehouse is staffed by robots, but that principle remains the same. This naturally constrains the work that needs to be done by way of implementation, and as such "if you've built one piece of software to manage a warehouse, you've built them all". Non-technical teams and leaders can oversee and manage implementation for bespoke *customisation of off-the-shelf systems*.

The untethered nature of this purely bespoke work creates enormous scope for problems, and I would say that I believe it is only possible to outsource bespoke software development work if you are yourself a software developer. We spoke before in Chapter 7 about fractional (i.e. consulting) chief technology officers. I would say that you should not attempt pure bespoke work without a fractional CTO, and I say this because I have never seen it work effectively. I say "effectively" because the problems that occur fit into certain classes of problems. The common problems I would call out here is that (a) non-technical customers end up paying too much, (b) the output is almost always designed to satisfy a need now, and is not designed to satisfy the needs of the organisation in 5, 10, 15 years, and (c) the solution is never properly mated to the business operations that underpin what the software is doing. You can only effectively use outsourced software developers to *augment* an existing technical execution effort, not to *be* that technical execution effort. This is the classic situation of out-source things you don't want to get good at; in-source ("in-house") things you do want to get good at.

Bespoke software development is usually done to power some new business innovation – an entrepreneurial team sees a gap in the market and decides to deliver a technical solution to that problem space. What newcomers to this work do is that they build backwards – they build an app (or a website, or a platform), and then design the business underneath it. This is a much more complex proposition than the actual process of building the product, and requires a much more long-term systems thinking approach than that initial product. Non-technical teams also tend to underestimate the need for flexi-bility within the product itself – and even that is not as easy as it seems because it's critical to strike the right balance between flexible and fixed because overly flexible solutions tend to not tightly track the customer needs and customer journeys, and are harder (more expensive) build, maintain, and support. The actual "business engineering" side also, weirdly, is harder because today we find that business engineering – the need to be able to rapidly innovate against customer journeys and customer experience – is a faster-moving field than software engineering because software engineering is more mature than business engineering. (For example, RevOps is emerging, complex, and necessary, and brand new, but the way people build and package apps hasn't fundamentally changed in ten years.)

It's even more essential in pure bespoke development that anyone you outsource to is a genuine delivery partner of the organisation and is invested into the organisation's success at owning and operating that software. A pure bespoke development house is not someone you randomly find in a spam outreach LinkedIn direct message, or via UpWork or Fiverr. It requires careful (and expensive) assessment of a competent advisory firm that is properly aligned.

To finish off, I should reiterate the importance of intellectual property transfer with pure bespoke development work. We covered this in Chapter 5, but there must be a process and mechanism for transferring IP at the correct points in the development cycle. Again from Chapter 5, it is absolutely critical to have some sort of escrow arrangement (and associated business continuity plans and procedures) whereby the critical failure of the outsourcing partner has only a minimal impact on your ability to continue to ship your solution.

Summary

In this chapter, I started by talking how I felt that bespoke software has the capability to deliver the best outcomes for businesses, but that it's relatively rare now to have a "pure bespoke" project when it comes to the types of system this book is about because the quality of the commercial off-the-shelf solutions tend to be so good now.

The mistake many organisations make now is stopping at implementing the COTS solution, missing out on significant opportunities. Regardless of what your organisation does, one thing remains true: it is utterly unique. The way all the pieces of your organisation fit together, your customers, your employees, and the network of organisations supporting you create a one-of-a-kind entity. The way to bridge this gap in modern businesses it to think hard about integration – try not to allow the business to deliver these little silos of data and capability, but instead think about building a "business operating system" that joins everything up together, intelligently.

Because it is my first love, I should summarise the matter of bespoke development. The most important thing to appreciate is that it is fantastically difficult to outsource software without having in-house IT decision-making capability. Outsourcing works to augment an existing team (which can just be a head, without engineers), but it almost always fails if a non-technical business just outsources without that in-house capability. That failure can be critical (i.e. it's just a waste of money), or it can be lacking in critical ways when you look out the medium and long terms.

Chapter 9

Dealing with Variations

The structure of the working method in this book is designed to help you avoid the number one toxic situation between customer and supplier that can occur when implementing complex IT systems project – the issue around "scope", or rather conflict about what's "in scope" and what's "out of scope".

When a customer and supplier come together for the first time to deliver a project, there is a big difference in perception. The supplier has built the system the customer wants many times before and has a very good idea of what the customer will get for their money. The customer has never built the system before and has no idea what they will get for their money. This creates an ideal environment for a conflict around scope.

The way to smooth this situation out is to get the parties closer together. The approach that I have taken in this book looks to get the customer as being more able to express the needs of the system from the organisation's perspective. Customers typically are not expert in expressing their needs well on a formal basis and are reliant on the supplier to facilitate expression of those needs. Problems occur when the supplier is either (a) not very good at that (and/or naive), or (b) is working to an agenda that has more to do with their commercial interests as opposed to the customers. In particular, this happens

DOI: 10.4324/9781003427766-9

when the supplier is desperate to sell (or is greedy to sell) – the dynamic here being to pick up the contract for the project and assume any problems can be fixed as the project proceeds.

Ideally by being able to follow the process in this book, you will become good at expressing your needs, and you will do a good job of choosing the right supplier.

Even if you do have a good specification and choose a good supplier, it is still possible to end up with conflicts around scope. Scope conflicts occur when the customer wants something delivered, but the supplier feels it is not part of the work that was originally agreed. If the project is headed to a place where it is going to go very badly wrong, this is normally where the resentment that causes the breakdown in the relationship occurs. Back in Chapter 3 (The Shape of the Solution) we spoke about estimations, and specifically we discussed how the estimate was intimately tied to the profitability of the job. Any time the supplier is being pushed against issues with scope, there is a potential to erode profitability. Erode profitability too far and the supplier will eventually move into a place where the project is lossmaking. From there, resentment builds and conflicts turn into disputes.

However, as has been said several times as we've worked through the book, it is not possible to know with 100% accuracy what you are going to build before you have built it. There has to be some wiggle-room in the project in order that things that are either genuinely missed or only loosely known can be delivered. There will be some wobble, and the supplier will have baked in a buffer into their estimate to allow for variations.

What Are "Variations"?

Variations are small changes in the project trajectory that can be used to positively target the project to the point of value delivery that the organisation wants to achieve. The key word here is "small" – variations are not intended to plug up huge errors in the original project design. Think about a small pothole in a road that is an annoyance when you drive over it, as opposed to a massive hole in the road that would swallow your whole car.

By way of an example, getting halfway through the project and finding out that although you operate multiple warehouses, finding out that the system you've bought can only handle one is not a "variation". This is a massive error – and one that would have been fixed by operating an effective scoping exercise at the start of the project. On the other hand, getting halfway through the project and finding out one of your suppliers was moving from barcodes on labels to QR codes on labels would be considered by a variation as this was effectively unknowable at the beginning, but is now an obstacle to project delivery. For example, you might need to buy and configure new scanners that can read QR codes, or you might need to upgrade a module earlier than expected.

A bit like the double-slit experiment in quantum mechanics, variations only come into existence when they are observed. Yes, the supplier might have been thinking about changing their label format for six months, but the variation in your project only occurred when they told you – that is, when they observed it. This piece of logic tells you that it is absolutely critical to observe your project as it runs, which luckily in Chapter 6 (Project Management) we build out a proper observation and reporting framework to keep a close eye on the project as it runs. Effectively, this creates a culture within the organisation where everyone is naturally working to observe how the project is running, and through the project board and the project meetings, it should be easy to readily detect variations.

However, a key part of this is actually getting people to use the system with intent – and now we're looking back at Chapter 7 (Resourcing). This needs to be an actual genuine attempt to get people to go in and use the system for real (or as close to "for real" as possible), during development. We've previously discussed this idea of Type A and Type B activities, that is, the former being core activities related to the person's day job and the latter being extra stuff we need them to do for the good of the organisation and the project. (This sort of observation of the system is separate from formal testing, which we'll cover in the next chapter.)

For example, if one of the deliverables of the project is a new report for the finance team on credit control, the finance team will need to run and look at that report, and they'll need a way of telling the project board whether it works or not. (And the project board will need to listen …) The finance team might look at that report and declare that it needs to show the PO numbers related to past due invoices. That again is also a fairly decent example of a variation – because it should be relatively cheap (i.e. won't take much time, won't erode the supplier's profitability, etc.) to implement. As a rule, if you find small variations close in proximity to the time the engineer is actually delivering the feature the simpler (cheaper) the change is to do. To use the housebuilding analogy we've dipped into throughout this book, it's easier to swap out the last course of bricks that you added to the wall as opposed to swapping out bricks that are ten courses deep. (Software engineering has a deeply "accretive" effect, meaning that each part is built on the last part – it's more like building a wall than one might expect.)

Like all good variations, the earlier on you see them the better as it tends to be the case that the earlier you spot something is wrong, generally the cheaper it is to fix. I'll reiterate a previous example – imagine an architect who designs a house, but for some reason produces a drawing that is a mirror-image of the intended implementation. It's way cheaper for that error to be spotted before the builder starts building it as opposed to having to knock it all down and start over.

Variations as Opportunity

My philosophy professionally and personally is to look at every problem as an opportunity. (But then, the think I like doing more than anything else is solving problems, so you better hope I like it.) As the system is built, reports from the field will come in, and each one will look like a problem. "The supplier is moving from barcodes to QR codes", "This report doesn't include PO numbers, so I need to manually go through and cross-reference", and so on. It helps a great deal to look at every problem with regards to system performance as it's being built as an opportunity.

As has been said a decent number of times before in this book, it's impossible to know what you are going to build until you have built it. Some "misalignment" between the perception of what needs to be built and what is actually being built is a fact of life – correcting this misalignment through a proper variations process is an opportunity to build exactly the system that you want.

It is 100x preferable to find problems with the system whilst it is being built and remedying those problems during the engineering process than it is to go back and fix things post-delivery.

Variations as Risk

A good thing about being able to detect that variations need to be made is that it means you are able to listen – that is, you have the project board and oversight processes set-up correctly. However, it's important not to be glib about variations. I've looked to be positive about variations in these pages, but every variation does at its core indicate a mismatch between the designed solution and the implemented solution. Each variation represents a mistake in the original design – and we have to be forgiving of these (after all, pencils come with erasers on the end) – but every mistake does represent a risk. For example, if the supplier changes from barcodes to QR codes and vendor doesn't have support for this coming onstream until six months after the project is supposed to be delivered, then we have a problem.

We therefore want to have variations that are "forgivable", and not be at home to variations that are anything more than that.

First, variations can be indicators that the scope and specification are just poorly done, that the specification and requirements are incomplete and inaccurate. As a first-time customer of this process, you may not be well-placed to gauge this. This is where you need to get the supplier to indicate to you whether the variations that are coming up are regular, expected variations or not. If they are not, it's important to catch this early and – politics aside – you may have to stop and reboot the project. We've seen the principle of spotting things early many times, if something is going wrong – if you are building that house in the mirror image of how its supposed to be built – it's far better to stop building it and reset.

Second, variations can be an indicator of lacklustre stakeholder involvement. Stakeholders need to provide input both at the design stage and at the implementation stage. If their involvement was poor at the design stage, that links back into the above point – maybe you're not building the right thing. However, during implementation stakeholders are able to quash little/small issues during implementation. If they are doing their job right, you may not even know that they *are* variations. For example, if the CFO is taking to the engineer about the credit control report and the CFO mentions that PO numbers need to appear, the engineer may roll that feedback in as part of their standard implementation flow. The project board may not even hear about it, and this is the ideal case – micro-corrections being made during development that do not push out project timelines. If that's not happening, perhaps the stakeholders are not spending enough time getting their hands' dirty.

Third, variations can be an indicator that the project is poorly managed. This links into the above point, but is one level higher in the project hierarchy. Variations come from somewhere – and they grow in size and stature if left unmanaged. If variations are getting complex and hairy to manage, it can be an indication of poor project management, or rather the project management regime that you have set-up to oversee the project needs some tuning.

Fourth, we also have to be careful that some suppliers might be overly accommodating to variations. Some suppliers will just take on too much and "people please" to the extent that they can ironically damage the project success by taking too much of a "customer is always right" mindset and absorbing all the problems and all the delays themselves. Like in any relationship, the healthy thing to do is to have boundaries and push back when appropriate – some suppliers don't have boundaries and will just let the project flub along and get later and later and more divergent form the original plan under a mistaken belief they are doing the right thing.

Finally, one variation is a strong indicator that more variations are coming. We spoke about this idea before of "see one, think two" – that is, if we're driving along and a rabbit runs in front of the car, what's the chances that it's being chased by a fox? Don't assume that if you're dealing with a variation – even if it's a large variation – that this is the last one. In Chapter 11 where we talk about projects that are actively failing, the Number 1 reason why projects fail is because of out-of-control variations (this itself being related to issues with scope and/or original requirements), these being caused by something fundamentally wrong in the project.

Specifics of Managing Variations – "Change Management"

Back in Chapter 6 when we looked properly at project management, we sketched out the pattern for how project management should be done in terms of having a board and needing to run the meetings, but we didn't look at any specific artefacts – that is, the documents used to manage the project. In reality, because you as the customer are looking to *oversee* the project and not *manage* the project, the artefacts should be designed and chosen by the supplier, not you. As most readers of this book would likely have been involved in projects before, you will likely know what good and bad project management artefacts look like. However, I do want to go into specific artefacts related to handling variations as by definition most readers of this book would not have managed complex IT systems projects before.

When dealing with variations, you can broadly divide the work into two types of variations. There are major variations, which can be thought of as: "oh, I wish we'd thought of that sooner". (Some of those can be genuinely heart-stopping.) There are minor variations, which are small adjustments to the project course that you can make much more easily. It's important to size the change management process to suit both of these types, in effect running two systems for minor and major. For example, you do not want your minor change process so rich in ceremony that the bulk of the labour goes into managing the project. You do want your major change process so light that you lose the ability to use the variation's existence as a reflection point to consider whether other deeper problems exist. It's generally easier to size the major process than the minor process, but one risk of the minor variations is that you miss the "death by a thousand papercuts" issue where your project's issues are expressing themselves through hundreds of tiny things that are wrong.

Key to managing the minor variations is knowing that time and opportunity to fix minor variations will be baked into the project estimates. Recall the example that we cited earlier about having the CFO review the credit control report and them feeding back to the engineer that the PO numbers needed to appear on the report. The engineer will be expecting to make this sort of change as part of their initial implementation – the trick in this case is to make sure you can get the CFO to get eyes on the report early, the process of managing the engineer's changes is less important. It's likely that this change does not even need to be logged, as it's just part and parcel of the initial development effort.

Let's look now at a suggested change management process, and from there we can deal with the issue of determining whether a variation is minor or major. To reiterate, this is just an illustration to help you understand what change management process your supplier may be using – albeit the supplier may (non-ironically) vary their process to suit this if there are previously missing parts of this that may work for you.

There are seven parts to this process:

1. Change request form,
2. Change impact assessment,
3. Change approval,
4. Change log,
5. Change request tracker,
6. Change control plan,
7. Post-implementation review.

Change Request Forms

The first thing that needs to happen is that a change needs to be notified. In order for there to be a notification, there would have been some informal conversations as to the fact a change is needed, and it's critical that there is a process to transform that informal conversation into a formal request. This will take some discipline to do but it's hugely important.

As we'll see in Chapter 11, and as I have hinted it in previous chapters, most projects fall apart because of issues with scope. If you end up in a legal dispute with your supplier, the one thing that you will wish you had is a robust record of how that scope flexed and changed over time. I have seen horrendous problems in disputes where parties ended up court arguing over scope without a strong specification and without any evidence of how the scope changed. The worst thing you can do is have all of the scope changes "recorded" in ephemeral Teams calls that no one can go back and examine.

The easiest way to do this is to have a change control form that simply sets out what change needs to be done, and why. This can then be stored along with all of the other project artefacts for consideration in the next project meeting. (You can obviously convene a special meeting if the matter demands it.)

Change Impact Assessment

Once you have recorded the change using the change request form, you can now turn your attention to assessing the impact of the change. With an outsourced provider, there is a strong chance that this activity can get somewhat tunnel-visioned, that is, the supplier ends up fixating on cost and you end up fixating on paying for it. The reality is that making change to software systems is more than just creating a new work item and sticking a price tag on it. You can intuit this if you imagine an in-house software project where costs are more fixed – those sorts of changes are not just measured in terms of time, they are measured in terms of strategic outcomes. It is important to look carefully at where that change gets you in the long-term, not just what the short-term fix is.

For example, what's the long-term impact of having one supplier change their barcoding format to QR codes? What's the long-term impact of needing PO numbers on credit control reports? There will always be some deeper meaning behind the change – in particularly you should consider every change in terms of short-term versus long-term, direct versus indirect impact, and positive versus negative. It's worth putting together a template where these headings are specified down so each time a change is being considered, that template can be used and you can be certain that these various factors are being included.

Do be careful though to consider the balance between minor and major changes. For example, a change that was brushed off as a minor change may end up in reality being a major change. (Obviously if what was thought to be a major task ends up being a minor task all you've wasted is planning and management time.) There isn't much you can do to legislate against major issues masquerading as minor issues – it comes down to skill in spotting them.

Change Approval

Any change that can be requested obviously needs to be approved (or denied). If the change is approved, you will feel the impact of the cost of resources – certainly in terms of time, but perhaps also any approved changes in cost. It's very important that any changes in the cost profile of the project are properly recorded and trackable, as you'll need to rely on this if something does go wrong.

For example, if there is a dispute, later changes in the scope are likely to become material. You will need to be able to properly refer back and track that change all the way from query, through the change (re-)specification above, then through to approval and payment. What is important is being able to lay out the story clearly, in a set structure, as this (a) gives you and any expert you get to support you the ability to show that you've had sufficient oversight to be the "responsible adult in the room", and (b) you won't need to dig around in emails and in your mind for half-remembered conversations to give you a clear picture as to what's happened.

Change Log, Change Request Tracker, and Change Control Plan

I've lumped the last three documents together, again from the perspective of someone who just needs to know what a good change management system looks like, you just need to know what they are, not how to run them effectively.

Any process requires a logging system for tracking progress, and the first two documents here seem similar but are different. The change log is your record of what changes were made. Coming back to the earlier point, this log is critical if you ever need to go back and retell your story about how and why the project got to the state that it is in. It's an immutable document – that is, it's an audit record that doesn't change. The change request tracker on the other handle is a mutable, active document that records the active change requests. This is document is important because it helps people understand why the project is varying. It may seem silly, but non-technical people who are involved in complex projects – imagine stakeholders or other resources that are informing the project trajectory – often don't maintain a strong mental grip on the project, and this can lead to a lot of "um, why did we do this?"-type questions. This tracker helps you and them understand and keep top-of-mind why the project is "off-piste" in the way that it is. (Although ideally you shouldn't need to use the tracker too much as we're trying to design and operate the project so that the number of trackable/major variations is kept to a minimum.)

The change control plan is a separate document/template created on a per-variation basis that is designed to hold the details of the change as it's being done. The construction of this document must be compatible with the other artefacts that have been detailed in previous chapters – that is, it must contain a specification of the work to be done together with mapped stories that describe the totality of that specified work. Alongside that there needs to be the formal plan of the resource allocation. In a normal change management process, there always is this detail around the "when" and "who" – that is, time and resource allocation. However, in this process because variations can so often be the precursor to dispute, it's worth also being able to document the "how much" in a way that's linked to these change control plans. (For example, that invoices are to be raised against the work, and for how much.) However this data can be sensitive, so you may need to record this in a separate document (or even in a separate log).

Post-implementation Review

Philosophically, I don't believe in processes that cannot be reviewed. (In general the IT industry likes to always be on a path of "continuous improvement in competence".) A post-implementation review is always important in any project, but it's worth doing a kind of "micro-review" at the end of each variation implementation because of the risk that variations can be an indicator that a project is going off-the-rails. Each implementation should therefore end with a meeting to check-in on how the variation was addressed, the minutes of which should be recorded.

Internal Communications (and "PR")

We haven't spoken much about internal communications around project delivery so far in this book, and this is because the size of project this book covers tends not to warrant it. In a very large organisation where there is a major system rollout – think a hospital where a new electronic patient record system is being rolled out – internal communication is a whole topic in its own right. In our project, what's likely is that management staff will be on the project board, and almost through a process of osmosis the people who report into them will end up with sufficient knowledge as to what is going on. (It's also reasonably likely that because those staff lower down in the organisation have a job to do, they may not be particularly interested in the project – and if they are interested it's usually because they are looking to be rescued from some operational difficulties that the new system is designed to alleviate.)

However, rolling out a new IT system is nearly always political – by definition, an IT system is change, and a default position to change tends to be one of a kind of "wary hostility". As such, there is a balancing act where management need to keep a lid on a certain amount of unrest with regards to system implementation. Where management often lose their grip on matters related to timescale slippage, and timescale slippage in an otherwise well-run project is always down to variations.

So whilst on a project of the scale and scope we're discussing in this book you don't need a separate "internal communications function" that you might see on rollouts that operate on a larger scale, you should bear in mind that variations popping up and needing active direct management often come with this additional baggage of needing to do some capable comms management internally. When you do this, it's important to consider this issue we discussed earlier about "see one, think two". If you are seeing one complex/ major variation, remember that it's likely more will be coming along down the line. Tune your communications accordingly – in particular the last thing you want to do is be caught saying that this change is the "last change", and we're "nearly done" because if you're having to manage variations, it likely isn't the last one.

Summary

Dealing with variations is essential because it is effectively impossible to completely and accurately define every feature of the project up-front – things will "come out of the woodwork" as the project progresses. The supplier and customer have different objectives when it comes to variation though. The supplier will "bake in" some leeway to allow for variations, but when variations become deviations from the scope, profitability can become squeezed, an issue that can become political.

Variations should not be used to fix major errors in the original project design. They should be more like small pot-holes in a road rather than massive holes that would cause significant damage, and detecting variations early is crucial because it allows for cheaper and easier fixes. Observing the project closely through an observation and reporting frame-work, as discussed in Chapter 6, helps identify variations promptly. Additionally, encouraging stakeholders to actively use the system during development facilitates the early detection of variations.

Remember, variations should be seen as an opportunity to align the designed solution with the implementable solution. By actively managing variations, you will end up with the system you truly want and minimise risks and conflicts along the way.

Chapter 10

Testing

By the time we've got to this chapter, congratulations, you almost have a working system. Now we just need to make sure that what you have bought works.

Where Testing Fits

Years ago, I went to Boeing's Everett Factory, which used to be where they made 747s. Whilst the testing process in new airliner designs is massively complex, the way that individual, complete planes are tested is weirdly chill. They build the plane, the customer's test pilots pop over to Everett, takes the plane out for a flight, and if it's signed off the customer's flight team arrives at the factory and flies the plane immediately to the first scheduled airports to pick up customers. That airliner is then in continuous use 24 hours a day until it's retired. This talks volumes about the quality of individual assessment phases used during the construction of the plane, but key to out discussions here is this point: "testing comes at the end".

However, from our perspective where we are operating a far, far less rigorous engineering process, testing at the end leads to a problem if we have not detected problems with the system during development. In this

 DOI: 10.4324/9781003427766-10

book, I've looked to set out a way of building the solution so that there is much more rigour, and as a result this nightmare scenario of getting to the end and funding you have bought a hunk of junk is substantially less likely.

Testing needs to be done throughout the process, and this means that the project board has to cajole the stakeholders to lean in to the test process as the project runs. The report that the CFO specified has to be looked at and tested as the engineer is developing it so that problems with that report are found and varied using the methods in the last chapter as opposed to six months later. There are all sorts of problems that can occur when there is a big disconnect in time between "doing" and "testing" – one that's less obvious to non-technical people is that engineers tend to forget everything about what they've built the second they start building the next thing. (If an engineer has to go back and work on something that they last touched months ago, the effective process is reverse engineering what they built.) There is also a sequencing problem in that if they project is supposed to be delivered in, say, April and the bulk of the testing happens the week before and three months remedial work is discovered, that project will slip. It is critical to test well and to test early.

Test Environments

There are very few absolutely cast-iron rules when it comes to systems engineering, but one of them is: "don't build in production". What this means is: "don't do you actual engineering in the final systems that the customer is actually using".

The reason for this is obvious – bugs don't just magically appear; bugs are a result of the engineer making a mistake. A mistake in an operational computer system will have a commercial impact, and this commercial impact can be benign or it can be most definitely *not* benign. As a result, we get what is this practically the only unbreakable rule in software engineering – that things are tested, proven, and signed off in test environment before they are pushed into the so-called "production" environment. (The flip side of this is where we get that other well-trodden software engineer trope which is the utterance: "Strange, it worked on my machine!")

Any system engineering effort requires three environments – the development environment (a small environment that the engineer has on their own machine on which they work), and then a test environment and a production environment. The test and production environments in an ideal work should be parallel, identical copies, but for the most part here close enough to identical is good enough. The engineer does the work on their own environment, and ultimately pushes to test where a test process is undertaken. If that test process is successful and signed off, the build is pushed to production. The key part is that any change has to go through this process, even if the solution has been previously rolled out.

The challenge in outsourced IT systems development is that the test environment is expensive. In particular, the vendor will require your supplier to buy licenses for testing and production, and this cost ultimately has to find its way down to you.

During the initial systems development process, this is a slightly "cleaner" proposition because you and the supplier are engaged in a longer-term, structured process to produce a thing, and during that process there is no such thing as "production" because the system has not yet been commissioned (as in "brought into life"). What will usually happen is that part of the engineering work will be spinning up that initial production environment, but practically that will be used as test. There are only two environments – development and "quasi-production", but there is still the separation. It is possible to get away with having just two environments all the way until final commissioning if the system is small and/or modular enough. You only *need* a test environment if there is a chance that changes you want to make affect production *data*, that is, that system has ever been used for anything that can be traced back to a commercial activity of some kind. What will tend to happen practically is that the project will naturally move from "dev to quasi-production" flow to the more proper "dev to test to production" flow, in particular, because most projects do not operate on a "big bang" approach but will be rolled out in a more phased way.

There is a key point where the project can get unstuck. Selling a customer (i.e. you) on a test environment is (a) difficult to explain, and (b) costly. These two things can derail a sales process, so it can be safer for the supplier to err on the side of optimism around not needing a test environment. This exposes you to risk in two ways – (a) you can get landed with a big unexpected bill for a new environment (which is not cheap) or (b) the supplier will try and corral and fudge the risk rather than cause you direct annoyance.

What the supplier must do is ensure that from the beginning their part of the architecture and design of the solution engineering works includes rolling out of this testing environment. You will see part of this cost come down to you as the customer, however, some suppliers just mash this cost up indirectly within the estimates. As such, in situations where test environments are not broken out separately in any documentation, you'll want to get them to illuminate where costs related to test environments are having their impact.

This covers the situation around test environments during that initial commissioning, but there is another problem with testing environment related to maintenance, in that in an ideal world that test environment has to stick around throughout the life of the system because if any changes need to be made, those changes still need to go through the "dev to test to production" flow. You as the customer therefore have two choices to make – you can either (a) bear the cost of operating a parallel test system to production throughout the system life or (b) have a strategy to produce a parallel test system whenever one is needed. It doesn't matter which – either adds cost and complexity – you just have to remember that having an engineer making changes directly in production (i.e. bypassing a test environment) is fantastically risky and in virtually every case a very bad move. Either way, it's critical to ensure that you have satisfactorily covered off this issue with your supplier.

"Who Does the Testing?"

The answer to this question is odd – I would say that if you're the customer, your perspective is that the supplier does the testing, but if you're the supplier, your perspective is that the customer does the testing. The proper answer is that both of you need to do the testing, but in different ways.

The best outcome is that both of you want the project to be successful, but – from the supplier's side at least – if the project is in conflict or there is an issue, one very easy thing for the supplier to push back on is that you, the customer, is responsible for final sign off. Most parties will conflate "testing" with "signoff", and whilst this is a relatively accurate assertion, there are subtle differences in each of these, which we'll come to. The biggest risk that you as a customer have is that if you are in dispute, the courts will regard a "signoff" as a significant signal that you were happy with the outcome, and this can have a big impact on how you can obtain remedy for any system issues. As such, you have to ensure that anything that looks like "signoff" is very deliberate.

To come back to my simple question with the odd answer above, it's important that you test the system because you need to know if it works. But, you're not an expert in testing, and – in fairness – testing is a complex, technical discipline in its own right and if you're an amateur team you're not going to be able to test to a level where a signoff is 100% safe. The supplier will be better at the technical business of testing, but they cannot test a solution to a point where it could be signed off because it's not safe for you to rely on their testing. You can assume best endeavours and good faith in their testing, but there are a million of things that can go wrong, not least of which is that they do not live and breathe your business like you and the rest of the senior team do. It's only the leadership of the commissioning organisation that can effectively sign off an implementation.

The way that I would describe and balance this is that there are two reasons to test, and both parties can do a properly contained and effective job of both of these elements. The first part of testing is confirming that what you have in front of you works. The second part of testing is confirming that what you have in front of you will continue to work. You as the customer can effectively do this first part, because it aligns with your skills and experience in understanding the organisation's operational domain and requires deep understanding of operational imperatives that the supplier will only (rightly) skim. The supplier can effectively do the second part because it talks to their skills in building something that is generally robust, that is, what you want to bring out of the process is their engineering experience.

To illustrate, imagine the example of the credit control report that the CFO that we've discussed a few times now. Imagine that rather than the error with the PO numbers not being shown didn't get spotted during development, so that needs to get identified and fixed at the testing stage.

The *omission* of the data is the issue, and this omission can happen in one of two ways. It can be (a) missed from the specification or (b) on the specification, but not delivered for some reason. In the former case, you'd be into a variations process as we discussed in the last chapter. In the latter case, there is an error in the delivery. (Both cases are frustrating because the project is supposed to be in a cadence where it's in the final run to delivery, and now work has to be done to unpack the feature and make the required change.) Coming back to the idea of who should identify that omission, that is down to the *customer* not the supplier. The supplier should make best endeavours to deliver to the specification, but it is ultimately down to the customer to approve and sign off the work. This is because, whilst you can expect the supplier to get to know you extremely well during the course of the project, they will never get sufficiently into the "domain" of how you operate as if they were a member of your own staff. It's ultimately up to you to assess the system's ability to fit into your operations.

The supplier does need to test, however, but it's on the same "best endeavours" basis. The supplier's test team will have the specifications and designs and will create test cases (more later), but you should not expect utmost rigour. Don't forget as well as the original specification you need to apply the newly created specification and design materials from any variations that you have had to deal with. These variations are likely to also require you to go back and change/ vary previously created test cases. For example, if a feature is removed, test cases related to that feature also need to be removed – but this may also have a knock-on effect on other test cases.

There will however be a whole bunch of testing that the supplier does that is hidden to you, but is an essential part of the process. There are categories of testing activity that relate to general fitness of the solution, which is orthogonal to your organisation's domain. To illustrate without going into too much detail, part of this work relates to the idea that "errors happen at the edges", and this is generally applicable to software, not just to your specific software.

To illustrate, imagine you have a feature that allows you to create an invoice with a value up to £1 m – that is, the specification gives that: "The value of the order MUST NOT exceed £1m". If you test and can create an invoice with a value of £250,000, you can pretty much assume that you'll be OK to create an invoice of £250,001 or £249,000. This is because none of those values are close to the edges. A good tester will try and create the following:

■ An invoice with value £1,000,000.00,
■ An invoice with value £1,000,000.01
■ An invoice with value £999.999.99
■ An invoice with value £0.00
■ An invoice with value £-0.01 (i.e. "minus one pence")

... that is, errors happen at the edges of the specification. If the user is able to key in an invoice amount freely, the good tester will also:

■ Enter a value of <nothing> (i.e. a blank string)
■ Enter a value of "sdfkhsdfkjh" (i.e. not a number)
■ Enter a value of "250000" (i.e. no annotations)
■ Enter a value of "£250,000" (i.e. with annotations)
■ Enter a value of "£250000" (i.e. with some annotations)
■ Enter a value of "£249.999,99" (i.e. with non-standard UK/US annotations)
■ etc.

This is the sort of testing that you should not expect to do, but the supplier should do because this sort of testing tests general fitness. This can be specific, however. In the case of PO numbers, the supplier may see examples of typical PO numbers used within the business, but can use their own experience to test the system with the other similarly typical PO numbers they may have seen in other projects. Overall, the supplier is looking to "flex and bend" the solution to see if it – literally – snaps. This is the sort of professionalised, structured testing that as a customer you should rely on the supplier to do. Fundamentally, it looks to reduce the total cost of ownership of the solution.

How to Test Well

Of the two types of testing that we've just illustrated – the sign-off testing that you do and the structured testing process the supplier does, there is more "professional rigour" on the supplier's side in that there has to be a defined process setting out how and what to test, and this rigour leads to certain process artefacts related to testing that need to exist. Like the last chapter on project management, it's not down to you to run this process, but it is down to you to oversee the process. As such, it's beneficially that you know roughly what a good testing process looks like. You should take steps to properly understand the supplier's test process, and you should look to reproduce a small, "pocket" version of this process for managing your own testing. (Your own testing process should also be structured.) You may also need to copy down some of the artefacts created by the supplier into your own organisation, for reasons that will become clear.

The trick with testing is that it needs to be repeatable, which means there needs to be a library of "test cases", each test case detailing a unit of operation, and the totality of test cases must cover the entirety of the solution. This may sound familiar as it's exactly the same approach that we set out for the functional specification itself – in both cases, there needs to be enough documentation to cover the totality of the solution.

The method used to writing test cases will vary, but they have the same fundamentals. They (a) describe the state of the system before the testing starts, (b) what steps constitute the test, and (c) describe the ideal state of the system once the testing ends. By way of a non-domain example, imagine starting a car:

1. **Before:** The engine is switched off.
2. **Steps:** With the user sitting the driving seat, the user DOES press the brake pedal and presses the "Start" button.

3. **After:** The engine is now switched on.

Then, for example you might write this test case:

1. **Before:** The engine is switched off.
2. **Steps:** With the user sitting the driving seat, the user DOES NOT press the brake pedal and presses the "Start" button.
3. **After:** The engine is remains switched off.

Hopefully, you can see that the point of the cases is to create a lot of small operations that together exercise the totality of the system. The purpose of having them written down is that you are then able to "regression test" the whole system whenever changes occur. One of the major problems when building software systems is that you can change one part of the system and make what you believe to be quite an innocuous change, and that change causes major problems in another part of the system because of occult/hidden interconnections within the system. As a result, even minor changes should properly result in complete, end-to-end regression testing. You cannot effectively do that without a proper library of test cases that can be used for this sort of regression testing.

To illustrate with a domain example, a test for this system may be:

1. **Before:** Goods are to be received into the warehouse. A purchase order showing the goods exists on the system. On examination, the purchase order shows that the goods have not been received. The boxes to be received exactly match the order – that is, the purchase order shows three boxes are to be received, and three boxes are to be received. The boxes are intact, have QR codes on them, and are otherwise good to receive.

2. **Steps**: The goods are received. The QR code on each box in the order is scanned with the hardware scanner
3. **After**: The purchase order now shows that the goods have been received.

Both you and the supplier need your own test libraries, although because of the different nature of testing roles these do not need to be shared. It is better not to share them as it can create an artificial reliance on the other party when that should not be there, although it can seem like there is duplication inherent in this arrangement. The reason for this is that the final sign-off – which we'll talk about in a moment – is commercially critical.

When you do a test run, it's important to log the output of the testing. This can be done using a spreadsheet. Each test case should have a unique identifier – this can just be a sequential number. Test cases can be deleted – for example, if features are removed. (This would be important if you need to go back over the logs as part of building up a picture of the trajectory of system development, for example if you do end up in dispute.) The log can just be a simple Excel or Google Sheets spreadsheet.

Signing Off Testing

Signing off your solution is the point at which you commit to putting your system into production use. Once the signoff is done, the effect is that the responsibility for it working properly moves from the supplier to you. As such, it is critical that you are certain the system works as expected/as required at this signoff point.

The risk to you as a customer is that signoff process is effective in saying that you are happy with what you have been given. If, over time, you work out that you are not in fact happy but the system that you spent all this time and money on is "a bit crap", your recourse against the supplier becomes much more difficult if they are able to turn up a document where you agreed that the system was fit for purpose, and a document indicating that you signed off on a system going into production is highly effective at showing that you believed the system to be fit for purpose. (We're going to talk more about legal action in the next section.)

The supplier is highly motivated to get to final signoff, because they can only complete invoicing and receive payment for the system once this point is crossed. If the project has also been difficult for whatever reason, they may well also approach this signoff wanting to "get you out of their hair" – again, this can add to the motivation to get to sign-off. In particular, you must be very careful to ensure that the signoff is agreed by the organisation, not done unilaterally by a member of staff who didn't have the buy-in of the whole organisation. (An employee can have be found to have apparent authority to do a thing and bind the organisation, even if the organisation's board would argue that they did not.) You can fix this problem by ensuring that everyone on both side knows and that it is agreed in writing that, for example, only the CEO is able to do the signoff. (The trick is to ensure the supplier knows that authority only comes from one source and one source only; you also need to evidence that they knew this explicitly.)

Given that the first "trick" is to ensure that both sides know only one person can do the signoff, the other second "trick" is to ensure that you know how to do a proper signoff. Happily, this is just a matter of running through the test cases that we defined in the previous section. (Of course, this process depends on your library of test cases being decent – that is, do they properly match the spec, do they properly match the system as built, and do they have 100% coverage.) The test log (see above) should be attached to any signoff documentation as well. Again, if there is a dispute what you want to be able to do is use the materials to build up a picture of the trajectory of development.

Once that's all done! Congratulations – you have a working system! Hopefully, you won't need the support sketched out in the next chapter, where we look at critical system failures…

Summary

In my experience, testing is (weirdly) overlooked in delivering the types of systems that we talk about in this book. Although the system is "tested" in virtually every case, there is a difference between "testing" and having a decently robust system for ensuring the system actually works. This starts by not assuming that all of the testing comes lumped at the end of delivery – testing in a continuous process.

What I'm arguing for in the way I've put this testing chapter is to make the testing process happen in a more collaborative way than typically happens. Your role as the customer is to test the operational domain – "does this system do what we need it to do". The supplier's role is to test that the solution is "generally robust", that is, that is has been delivered to a professional standard. Ultimately though, it is you the customer who is responsible for signing off the solution.

Chapter 11

Dealing with Failure

I was inspired to write this book because I wanted to help leadership teams that don't have access to IT leadership buy complex IT systems with confidence. Hopefully if everything has gone well, you only need the previous ten chapters, plus introduction, and you won't need this one.

Ten Reasons Why IT Projects Fail

Below, there are ten reasons why IT projects fail. Hopefully as you read these it will become clear how we've looked to ameliorate these risks through the steps and structure in the previous chapters. Here they are:

1. **Poor project planning** – this has been perhaps *the* theme throughout the book. Chapter 2 saw us develop a functional specification. Project management and resourcing were then covered in Chapter 6 and Chapter 7.
2. **Lack of stakeholder involvement** – we went through the importance of stakeholder engagement and how to get them engaged in Chapter 7.

DOI: 10.4324/9781003427766-11

3. **Inadequate requirement gathering** – the core of this was in Chapter 2, but a formal scoping exercise is critical here. We looked at scoping in Chapter 4 and Chapter 5.

4. **Scope creep** – scope creep should go away with effective requirements gathering and specifications, however, this also keys into variations, which we went through in Chapter 9.

5. **Poor communication** – poor communication should "go away" with efficient project management, which again we looked at in Chapter 6.

6. **Insufficient resources** – we have to consider both internal and external resourcing, which we went through in Chapter 7.

7. **Lack of skilled team members** – in this sort of project, the lack of skilled team members relates to those of the supplier, and again in this sort of project that's just an issue of how well you qualify the suppliers on your shortlist (and the supplier that gets commissioned). We talked about finding a supplier in Chapter 4, although this factor is one that you can only really "do your best with".

8. **Change management issues** – we look at variations specifically in Chapter 8, and in that we also look at building a process to handle change management.

9. **Ineffective risk management** – the central principle of the robust structure that this book focuses on is looking to improve risk management. As a result, risk management is covered in every chapter.

10. **Technology challenges** – this is a common failure point, but it's unlikely that a typical reader of this book will hit it. It refers to situations where projects are novel or "weird" – that is, projects that are trying to do something that not many groups attempt. Companies that supply outsourced IT projects rely on all the

customers on their base more or less doing the same thing – the more "out there" your project is, the higher the chance of failure. If you want to do something truly innovative, consider at a minimum bringing a fractional/consulting CTO into the business.

Hopefully from all that you can see how what we've looked to do as we go through this book effectively mitigates a lot of risk related to project failure. However, if you want to know if your project is in or is entering a failure state, you need to know what failure looks like. Let's look at that now.

Detecting Failure

It may seem odd to say, as it would be easy to assume the fact that a failure is occurring would be obvious, but the reality is that detecting failure in any type of complex project is difficult. The reason for this, in particular, is that IT projects take a long time to do, and the bulk of the work is being done by people who are doing something that looks arcane and strange from the outside. It is very easy to assume that everything is going OK, until it becomes apparent that things have not been going OK, and that perhaps things have not been OK for some time.

What can help is to visualise the project would be to imagine yourself on a desert island, and you can see some way off there is another desert island. You have a rowboat and you need to get from the island you are on to the other one. (You can make this imagining pleasant – e.g. you have lots of food, water, medical supplies, the weather is nice, i.e. in and of itself it's not a stressful journey.) When you set off, you know you can pull the oars of the row boat "n" times a minute, and we'll assume you're fit enough not to get particularly tired in the process. You expect the process of getting from A to B to take about an hour.

If something critical goes wrong, it would become very apparent – for example, if one of the oars broke, or the boat started to leak, or there was a tiger on the boat. That's not what a project failure is though, because project failures are much more insidious.

Firstly, imagine you are 15 minutes (25%) into the journey, and the island is in front of you. You measure the distance remaining and find that you are only 15% of the way into the journey. You are behind schedule – that is, you have not been making the progress you thought you would make in the time allotted. This is the first type of failure state, that is, you are going too slowly. The second type of failure state is that you have moved as far as you thought you would, but your estimate of where the destination island was turned out to be wrong. Thirdly, imagine you are again 15 minutes in, but this time the island is not in front of you, it's off to the right at a "2pm" position. This is the second type of failure state – you have wasted effort going in the wrong direction.

We already have a notion in common understanding of projects that they can "run late", and it's easy to brush off any lateness as not a problem. In this context, it's very important that we do not do this because if we have been managing the project properly, there should not be a concept of "late". We have specified the work, found the right supplier, designed everything, got the resources, and we are properly managing the project. Where is the "lateness" coming from? (And as in the above, is the lateness coming from a situation where we are going in the right direction but not achieving adequate "velocity", or are we going in the wrong direction?)

The nightmare situation that we are trying to deal with here is that there is a special type of project failure called a "death march", which not to mix metaphors is the equivalent of working the oars on our rowboat, but making zero progress. A death march project will never complete, and we'll talk about that more in a moment. For now, let's look at normal project failure.

The robust way that we have set out our project management regime (Chapter 6) should give us all the data we need to detect lateness, because we can use the data gathered by the project board to measure velocity. Velocity is the most basic—but happily is the most directly effective—measure that we can use to determine where we are. To keep the metaphor going, it's the equivalent of using a sextant to take a reading of our position. At the start of each sprint, we know what we want to do. So did we do what we wanted to do in that sprint? The answer to that question is a good enough measure of velocity. Short of some nightmare variation moving into view (e.g. an iceberg in our otherwise tropical waters), simply taking the total of everything we need to do and looking at how much we have done both in a sprint and in total tells us whether we're going to get to the end of the project in the expected time. The actual measurement is that simple.

The question then arises that if the velocity is not as expected, what is slowing us down? Practically, this can only be one of two families of issues – the resourcing is wrong, or the scope is wrong. Coming back to our rowboat analogy, these align. If we've only made 15% progress when we wanted to make 25%, we don't have enough resources. If we've moved as far as we should have done in real terms, but we're off course, we have the wrong scope. The latter case can be detected through variations. If we have a bunch of variations and slower velocity, we know that we have a scope problem. If we don't have a bunch of variations, but slower velocity, we either have a resourcing issue or an estimation issue. We can detect the difference between those by looking at the planned versus actual resource allocation. (It could be the case here that the delay is being caused by your own staff not being available to the supplier's staff – this case is easy to detect as the supplier is certain to raise this complaint.)

What's important here is that all of these metrics and determinations from them can be made even at the beginning of the project. The potential error will be huge (imagine firing a rocket at the moon and how a one-degree variation at the start of the journey has way more effect than the same one-degree variation one kilometre from the surface), but there is no reason why this can't be done from the start and it's important to do so. It is *far* better to detect problems earlier.

In terms of how you transfer this understanding into detection of failure, what you are looking for is a *pattern*. As I mentioned before, the nightmare scenario is not getting to the island at all. Project failure can occur even if you do get to the island. For example, you might get there late and exhausted. You might annoy all of your customers so much in how long it took you to get to the island that they've gone to a competitor. So much additional work was required in getting to the island, it cost twice as much as you thought it would to get there. The island might be full of tigers and not have enough food.

I'm being slightly tongue-in-cheek here, but project failures are a problem because, fundamentally, the organisation has wasted resources, usually money. The organisation can also miss opportunities – for example, not being able to get a product to market on time, frustrating a joint venture partner, etc. Or the organisation can miss a deadline that can cause it problems, for example, being fined because it failed to deliver a system to satisfy a change in regulation.

What we haven't spoken about is that if you can detect failure, you can fix it. If the supplier is not allocating the resources they are supposed to, you can apply pressure to resolve this. If your internal team is not leaning in to support a project, you can fix this however you feel it needs to be done. If the estimate or scope is wrong, this can get more problematic as this usually gets tied into some sort of loss – either you are going to spend more money with the supplier, or the supplier is going to fund more resources without benefitting from an increased profit.

Understanding What Happened

If you are running a project that has entered a failure state, it's likely that you will end up experiencing grief. It's shocking – everyone wants to be effective at their job, and a project failure means that you have presided over the organisation wasting time, money, and opportunity, usually all three. As you get to a point of conscious awareness that your project has failed, you will have both a personal need and a professional need to work out what happened. Building up a picture of what happened—and I can imagine this is seen as an unusual idea—is something that almost all smaller organisations struggle with.

Most organisations when running a project will do so on "autopilot". When the modality of the projects crosses from "successful" to "failed", this automatic, "going with the flow" nature comes back to bite them because one day they were looking at project going OK and then realise that at some point something happened to mean the project was no longer going OK. In our personal lives when something bad happens, whilst understanding how we got there is a matter of personal growth, it's optional for the individual to investigate and get to the bottom of what happened. An organisation cannot get away with this because failures are always serious and have to be understood via an investigative process. The feeling of being absolutely blindsided and desperately casting about trying to work out what happened is so common as to be the default position.

Because it is natural to resist consequences when things go wrong, the practical upshot of this is that failures have to be investigated and evidenced because any remedy that you push for in a failure situation will be resisted. Remember as well that the supplier will also be "waking up" to deal with a failed project and will be going through a similar process to yourselves in terms of understanding what actually happened. The difference is that you will likely come from a starting point of wanting your money back or other losses covered, and the supplier will come from a starting point of wanting to resist reaching to their pockets to pay you.

Separate to this, it is not possible to prosecute a claim without evidence. Similarly, it's not possible for the supplier to defend or make a counterclaim without evidence. The autopiloting nature of how projects can be run challenges putting together a properly evidenced case. This is why throughout this book I have encouraged creating a good number of evidential artefacts, such as minutes and logs. It's also very helpful to prefer modes of communication that are written – that is, email and enterprise instant messaging like Microsoft Teams and Slack are better than phone calls and video conferencing meetings. (As mentioned previously, WhatsApp is not great for this sort of communication as it sits outside of the organisation.)

Please remember as well that customers can sometimes want to make a claim against a supplier, only to find that they are not justified in doing so. To put it another way: a project failure is not automatically the supplier's fault.

In every situation that I have worked in where a project has failed, the root cause of the failure has always been retrospectively apparent much earlier on in the project than either party believed, but similarly it has always been very difficult to build up a picture of what happened throughout the course of the project because it is not common to create proper artefacts around project governance. A common problem is that upon realising a major failure has occurred, a key staff member or a few key staff members are fired – that is, it's common to find that "eyewitness" accounts of what happened disappear. People who are to any other measure capable and smart oftentimes voluntarily leave the organisation "magically" just before a project falls apart. (Regardless of how that person stops people readily available, without a set of evidence to back it up, eyewitness testimony in any field is always flaky.)

The nightmare situation is one where the management board of the organisation is ambushed by a project failure, and the person who was running the project and was closest to it has been fired, and there hasn't been proper design, planning, or management and the only artefacts you have are a loose collection of emails. To reiterate then, it's critical that project management artefacts are created, and created consistently throughout the course of the project, as without these it is practically impossible to retrospectively recreate a picture of what happened in the project in order to build a case to prosecute a claim against or defend a claim from the supplier.

Communicating Failure

In the section at the top of this chapter where we spoke about detecting failure, there was one common thread – the fact that there was less actual progress made against planned progress. This can happen in situations where there is a small blip (e.g. because of a variation, or a transient problem in resourcing such as someone becoming ill), or an outright failure. In either case, you'll need to communicate to other organisations and other stakeholders about the slippage. This usually ends up being quite an embarrassing process, and no one likes to do this. IT systems projects slip dates so often that it's something of a cliché. With a wise mind, however, communicating about slippage can be a way of detecting failure. Although the ideal position is that slippage and the potential for failure can be detected through project management activities, even if the project management process is not as effective as it should be, the fact that you are ending up communicating slippage should create an awareness in the team that something is going wrong. *A perfectly run project does not slip.* (Although the counterpoint is this: "no project is ever perfectly run, therefore all projects slip".)

There is a sort of political danger in this as well in that these sorts of communiques will nearly always be attributed as coming from the senior management team. If the project is on a slippery downward slope, it's quite common to end up emitting a series of messages that retrospectively, to the other tiers in the organisation, can make it look like the senior management team did not know what they were doing. This is because the messages tend to follow a cadence of "just a quick update, everything is fine, but there's a small delay" through to "another update, everything is very much not fine". People's perception being reality, it is important to carefully consider how these messages are drafted and with what frequency they are being communicated. It can be helpful to consider that the spin you put on things is sometimes a necessary evil.

Detecting a Death March

As noted above, "death march" projects are particularly insidious, and it's important to be able to spot them early because of the devastating effect that they can have on the organisation, and the careers of those within the organisation who happen to be their stewards. The outcome of a death march project is effectively a total loss of the resources that went into it, plus missed opportunity, plus enhanced risk (e.g. missing compliance deadlines). The next steps after a death march project are usually to "rip it up and start again". It's bad.

Sadly, despite the optimism in the headline for this section, it's not possible to detect a death march project before it happens. What you are relying on is a professional who knows how to put together an IT systems project seeing enough red flags to put the brakes on before the project starts, and/or being able to detect red flags very early on in the project. (Although if you detect that many red flags early on, you can then struggle with stopping the project because the person who is at this point a whistle-blower is likely not going to be listened to because the organisation is very gung-ho and confident at this point.)

For an organisation without in-house IT leadership, you are reliant on the supplier to advise on matters related to project design and project inception. (This has one positive aspect to it in that if the project does ultimately fail by becoming a death march project, you are likely much more able to build a case against the supplier because they have a duty of care to the organisation in the advice that they give.)

Red flags at project inception that can lead to a death march failure are:

1. **Deadlines are unrealistic** – the supplier should not allow this because they would tend to sequence deadlines in their own favour. However, a desperate supplier may overpromise;
2. **Insufficient resources** – again, the supplier should optimise resources in the same way they sequence deadlines. However, again a desperate supplier may overpromise;
3. **Improper specification and scope** – in this case, we saw in the first part of this book how we were working hard to ensure we have a good specification and scope;
4. **Overconfidence around novel ideas** – the parties are trying to do something that is novel and weird, but they are overconfident. This one is quite insidious as it's reasonably easy for two parties to end up joining forces convincing each other that they can deliver the undeliverable.

If we are looking at red flags further along in the process, there are some indicators that you at a minimum need to get a tighter grip on the project, and at a maximum indicate that the project is going to fail:

1. **Lack of ability to regain control of project velocity** – *this is what a death march project is*, so if you are able to both detect the velocity is out of control, and that you cannot seem to do anything about it, a major problem is occurring;

2. **Stakeholders remain consistently unengaged** – this means that those outside the project are not believing in your vision, but they are doing that through the intuition that yours and the project board's vision will not deliver the right outcome for them (and by extension, the organisation). that is, they are telling you that you are wasting your time;

3. **Ignoring feedback or warnings** – this requires someone on the board who will keep pushing when they feel the board are not heeding input that they do not want to receive.

In summary, death march projects are singularly disastrous, but usually the root cause for these types of projects that we are talking about in this book can be traced to a supplier that turns out to be particularly incompetent. What will turn the project into a death march project is your organisation being unable to detect and resolve this incompetence. In this book, we've worked hard to make a good supplier selection, get the project set-up as well as can be, and from there executed and delivered as well as it can be. You would have to be profoundly unlucky to follow all these steps and still end up with a death march project.

Supplier Insolvency/Bankruptcy

Talking about being profoundly unlucky, we should talk about one aspect of project failure that keeps me awake at night – that of the supplier going insolvent or bankrupt. The reason why this keeps me awake at night is because (a) it's utterly out of your control and (b) you cannot legislate against it.

I have lost track over my time doing this of customers who are more confident about the ability for a project to survive supplier bankruptcy than the reality that this situation ideally demands. The primary problem is one of intellectual property (IP). As discussed in Chapter 5, the supplier will almost certainly retain ownership of the IP until it is explicitly transferred. (Also mentioned in Chapter 5 is the fact that I am not a lawyer – you should seek proper legal advice on these issues.) Although this book is not written with any jurisdiction in mind, the general principle wherever you are is that any property of the insolvent business will pass to a third-party administrator. This property will include the intellectual property that makes up your system. At a minimum, this gives them the power to gain injunctive relief should you do receiving any benefit from that property whilst it remains in their ownership and/or they can make a claim for such if there is dispute or confusion over the current state of ownership.

A secondary issue to that – and this is the one that tends to trip most people up – is that any ability for the supplier to pay their staff's wages will halt your project with immediate effect. You can have the nicest and best relationship in the world with the supplier's staff, but if they are not being paid to do the job, you may well find that resource – along with all the skills and experience that goes along with it – becomes suddenly unavailable.

There are then a wealth of other issues that can come from being in a relationship with a failed or failing commercial entity. For example, the supplier may have put in an order for licenses for your project with their own suppliers, which they have not paid for, that their supplier may now claim that you cannot use. (And you may well have paid the invoice for those, it's just the cash was sitting in the supplier's bank account – and is now under the control of the administrator.)

Regardless of any eventual outcome, anything happening that is so foundational to the supplier will cause delays in the project.

A lot of these problems can be sorted out – it is unlikely that you will end up in a protracted dispute with the administrator because administrators are typically both sensible and efficient, but their timescales are their timescales and are more likely than not incompatible with your project plan. If the project is actively failing, the supplier experiencing a broad commercial failure can be most difficult indeed because you now have to triangulate the administrator into any remedial action.

I said before that you cannot legislate against supplier insolvency or bankruptcy. This isn't quite true; you cannot legislate *completely* against this eventuality, but there are things that you can do. Having the intended handling of intellectual property is critical. Having escrow agreements in place are also essential so that any administrator is clear what needs to be done when they are appointed. What you likely don't need to deal with up-front is that you do always have the option to directly engage any staff of the suppliers on a contract to complete the work themselves. You may have to deal with "non-poach" clauses in any agreement; then again, it is likely any agreement automatically fell away on appointment of the administrator anyway. (Again, your mileage may vary—ask your lawyer—but I have seen this approach of directly enga-ging a supplier's staff work extremely well before.)

Disputes: Arbitration, Technical Project Mediation, Court Proceedings, and Insurance

We went through a good amount of detail on disputes and arbitration in Chapter 5, but we should tie up the related loose-ends here. The reason why we looked at this first early on in the book was so that we could orientate your thinking such that you would have an eye on what might happen if the project failed. In particular, the major problem you have if you end up in court with your supplier is that whilst you might get your money back, you won't get a working system. It's clearly far more powerful to avoid failure in the first place as opposed to being able to—perhaps—back out some of the misspent money some months or years after delivery was supposed to take place.

The best solution if you have a failing project, in my view, is that of technical project remediation. However, this is a service that is very hard to find as not many companies or independent consultants offer it directly. (I should say that this is a service that I do provide, but even I don't put it front and centre on my website at www.mbrit.com.) The beauty of this type of service is that it looks to reboot and fix a failing project before it becomes an abject failure, and if the project is an abject failure it can help the parties build up a picture of what happened and get to a better solution sooner.

Like all legal disputes, it is usually better to resolve matters through mediation, rather than just jump into having a judge decide for you what happens.

Lastly, on this topic, do not underestimate the power of having the supplier use their insurance. This is what they purchase insurance for, and it is far too easy for a supplier to convince themselves out of making a complaint. Cooler heads often prevail when insurance companies get involved in matters.

Summary

In an ideal scenario, the previous ten chapters and the introduction to this book would be sufficient, and this chapter would not be necessary. However, things do go wrong. Where things get tricky is that you don't necessarily know the project is going wrong until you are well within the teeth of failure. An early system warning that you can rely on to detect any problems in the beginning stages is critical – a key part of this is being able to detect any changes in velocity; this is your best indicator of concern.

If we know a project is failing, we can do something about it. There are other considerations to make when a project has failed. For companies whose core business is not IT systems delivery, the biggest issue with outright failure is being able to build a picture of what failed that can be used in any remedy with the supplier. Projects tend to operate with very "ephemeral" outputs and artefacts that make it genuinely hard to look back and work out what happened when. Producing better outputs—and putting them somewhere safe so that you can find them again—is the best route you have to achieving remedy in the event of failure.

Chapter 12

Lessons from Fred Brooks[1]

In 1975, a project manager at IBM called Fred Brooks wrote a book called *The Mythical Man-Month*. The book is a series of essays on the topic of IT systems engineering, and it is so good and so important that even today it still remains relevant and is still required reading for engineers.

Given that the audience of this book are not engineers, it's unlikely that any reader of this book needs to read it in its entirety, but there is a common mistake that non-engineers make that happens to be referenced in this title of this book, but actually ends up being the second essay. For this reason, I wanted to summarise 9 essays from this book, illustrating how they relate to the content you've read. (I won't include all of the essays, just those that are relevant.)

Essay 2: "The Mythical Man-Month"

The "too long; didn't read" version of this essay can be summed up thusly:

Nine women can't make a baby in one month.

DOI: 10.4324/9781003427766-12

Easily the biggest misconception that I see non-technical people make is that you can increase a project's velocity by adding in more people. This isn't the case for the reason that as you add in more people, intra-team communication becomes exponentially harder and the effort required to coordinate new and old team members, and triangulate them into communications outweighs individual contributions.

You can, of course, add resources to a project team – however, it is an error to assume that these resources increase velocity, at least at the same rate at which you add people. There are diminishing returns. However, there may be benefit in adding in other resources that have *ancillary* involvement in engineering effort. For example, you may increase the number of trainers in order to smooth out bumps in the adoption of a project.

Realistically, try to avoid asking the supplier to add in more people if the project is experiencing delays, as it won't help. Similarly, if it looks like they are suggesting this approach to add velocity to a late project, pass them a copy of Brooks' book.

Essay 3: "The Surgical Team"

In this essay, Brooks compares the collaboration and dynamics of a surgical team to the ideal characteristics of a software development team. He highlights the need for a small and focused team that consists of highly skilled individuals who possess complementary expertise. Just as a surgical team relies on specialists with distinct roles, such as surgeons, anesthesiologists, and nurses, a successful software development team should have members with specialised skills, such as programmers, designers, and testers.

Additionally, Brooks emphasises the significance of a cohesive team that works together towards a common goal. Like a surgical team, where trust, communication, and coordination are essential for successful outcomes, software development teams need to foster a culture of collaboration, open communication, and mutual support. The essay emphasises that the effectiveness of a team lies not only in the individual skills of its members but also in their ability to work harmoniously as a unified unit.

How this essay lines up is that non-engineers often think that teams are larger and more complex than they really are. You can do *amazing* things with teams of 3–4 people or even 2–3 people. But that team has to be cohesive and able to work well together to achieve a common goal.

Essay 5: "The Second-System Effect"

Brooks discusses how the second system, often built with the experience and knowledge gained from the first system, can suffer from excessive ambition and feature creep. He explains that the developers, driven by the desire to address perceived shortcomings of the initial system, often succumb to the temptation of incorporating numerous new features and making the system unnecessarily complex. This overreaching leads to delays, cost overruns, and a system that fails to meet expectations.

The essay highlights the importance of disciplined and focused decision-making when embarking on the development of a second system. Brooks advises developers to carefully evaluate the needs and requirements of the new system, resisting the inclination to overcomplicate or reinvent the wheel. He emphasises the need for a pragmatic approach that builds on the lessons learned from the first system, while avoiding the trap of excessive ambition and feature bloat.

This is something that I have been bitten by in my career a number of times, and it's relevant here because often new systems come about because you have a homegrown, somewhat "janky" system that works and the organisation wants a new "v2" system. When you do this, it's crucial to (a) not overreach and (b) don't throw away the "magic" in the original system.

Essay 6: "Passing the Word"

Brooks highlights the complexity of software development as a major hurdle in passing information accurately and efficiently. He emphasises the need for developers to translate technical concepts into understandable terms and bridge the gaps between different disciplines. The essay underscores the importance of establishing a common language or glossary to standardise terminology and enhance clarity in discussions and documentation.

Brooks suggests several strategies to facilitate better communication. He emphasises the value of comprehensive and up-to-date documentation as a means of knowledge sharing. Additionally, he advocates for purposeful and well-prepared meetings to enable immediate feedback and clarification. The essay also highlights the significance of informal communication channels, such as water cooler conversations, in fostering collaboration and the exchange of tacit knowledge.

Nowadays, there tends to be far better interdiscipline communication between technical and non-technical teams. As of the time of writing, we're in something of a flux with regards to how office versus remote working will pan out, and with it the style of communication that we'll use. As with any complex endeavour, communication is key.

Essay 8: "Calling the Shot"

(This is "shot" singular, as in playing pool where one might call out which pocket the ball will land in.)

Brooks emphasises the difficulty of accurately estimating project schedules, particularly in the early stages of development when there is limited information available. He explores the inherent uncertainty in software development, as requirements evolve, unforeseen issues arise, and technological constraints come into play. The essay highlights the risks of making premature or overly optimistic projections, as it can lead to unrealistic expectations, schedule overruns, and overall project failure.

To address the challenge of calling the shot, Brooks suggests a combination of disciplined estimation techniques and ongoing project tracking. He emphasises the importance of breaking down the work into smaller, manageable units and basing estimates on historical data, experienced judgment, and thorough analysis. The essay emphasises the need for continuous reassessment and adjustment of estimates throughout the project, taking into account new information and emerging complexities. By adopting a cautious and iterative approach to estimating, teams can better navigate the uncertainties and increase the likelihood of delivering successful software projects on time.

To note, this essay was written 47 years ago, and talks even back then about the importance of properly specify and estimating a project. This still is not done well on the majority of IT projects. Hopefully given the first part of this book, your project's specification and estimation will be top-class.

Essay 9: "The Documentary Hypothesis"

In this essay, Brooks addresses the importance of thorough documentation as a means of communication, knowledge transfer, and project management.

The essay highlights the hypothesis that a system's documentation should be treated as a separate entity, independent of the code itself. Brooks argues that documentation should not merely serve as a description of the code but should be a comprehensive representation of the system, including design decisions, requirements, and user documentation. He stresses that documentation should be maintained and updated continuously throughout the project lifecycle to ensure its accuracy and usefulness.

Today, documentation related specifically to the system is much less important than it was 47 years ago. The reason for this is that engineers have always hated documentation and have applied two measures to the problem – one, they have resisted documentation at all costs, and two, they have designed the tooling used to build the systems as not requiring documentation. However, where this essay is relevant to the work covered in this book is that there does need to be a corpus of documentation that is maintained throughout the life of the project. The specification and designs in the first instance, then all of the documentation related to project execution, variations, etc.

Essay 10: "Plan to Throw One Away"

This essay focuses on the concept of iteration and the importance of learning from initial prototypes or versions of a software system. Brooks argues that it is often necessary to create an initial implementation, not with the intention of being the final product, but rather as a means of learning and refining the requirements and design.

The essay emphasises that the first version of a system is often flawed and does not fully meet the needs or expectations. Brooks suggests that teams should anticipate this and plan to "throw it away," meaning they should be prepared to discard or heavily modify the initial version. By doing so, teams can gain valuable insights and feedback, allowing them to refine and improve subsequent iterations.

Brooks advocates for an iterative and incremental approach to software development, where each iteration builds upon the lessons learned from the previous ones. He emphasises the importance of embracing change and adaptability in the development process, recognising that it is through the iterative cycle of building, learning, and refining that the best software systems are created.

This approach is incredibly valuable, but it's not *directly* applicable to the types of projects that we are considering in this book. The baseline assumption that "the first thing you build is trash" is correct, but we want the *supplier* to do their first, rubbish attempt in a way that doesn't affect us. We also need to consider the lesson from Essay 5 – the first system we build, our internal system, will be a bit janky and need replacing. That is the one that we "plan to throw away".

Essay 12: "The Whole and The Parts"

In this essay, Brooks emphasises the importance of balancing the focus on the entire system as well as its individual parts. He highlights that while attention to detail in individual components is crucial, it should not overshadow the need for a holistic understanding of the system as a whole. The essay argues that a successful software project requires a comprehensive perspective that considers the interdependencies, interactions, and integration of various components.

The essay also touches upon the concept of modular design, advocating for the creation of well-defined and independent modules that can be developed and tested separately. Brooks suggests that modular design enables teams to manage complexity, facilitate parallel development, and promote reusability. However, he cautions against excessive fragmentation of the system into small modules, as it can lead to integration challenges and hinder the overall system's functionality and efficiency.

What I want to do with this one is flip this on its head a little and think of the "whole" as the organisation and the "part" as the new system you are building. It's critical to think about the system you are building within the context of the organisation, the organisation's objectives and imperatives, and the wider systems in which it sits – society and the environment, suppliers, partners, and other stakeholders.

Essay 13: "Hatching a Catastrophe"

In this one, I only really want to highlight the title – as this is a truly brilliant way of summing up the importance of the work we need to do to run the project well.

The actual essay emphasises the importance of clear and efficient communication channels to avoid misunderstandings, conflicts, and delays. Brooks argues that without proper coordination, efforts can become disjointed, leading to project failures or catastrophic outcomes. He suggests that establishing effective communication and collaboration mechanisms, such as regular meetings, documentation, and shared understanding of goals, is crucial for successful project management.

For us, what we need to concentrate on are the risks inherent in building a complex IT system, and what we can do to ameliorate those risks.

Summary

That's it! Those are the key essays in Fred Brooks' book summarised. I'll take the essays that are still most relevant today, and hopefully, you can see that even 47 years after it was written, it's still hugely relevant, even to the work that we've done in this book.

Spookily, in the time between writing this chapter and getting it back for edits, I've had a week where I've had to use one Fred Brooks' titular essay with a client this week. It's amazing to me that 48 years after it was written, what is practically the only "textbook" the software industry has is still in use. It really is the case that nine pregnant women can't make a baby in one month – aka, you can't make a project move faster just by throwing more people at it.

I also had cause this last month to use "The Second System Effect" in consulting work with a different client. There is so much value to be had in building a "v2" of a working system – so long as that v2 isn't too radical. But I digress. The audience of this book will likely never have cause to read this book cover to cover, but it's critical that whoever you select as your vendor of choice to build your system has.

Note

1. Brooks Frederick P. 1995. The Mythical Man-Month : Essays on Software Engineering Anniversary ed. Reading Massachusetts: Addison-Wesley Publishing Company.

Index

Printed in the United States
by Baker & Taylor Publisher Services